TWO CUSHIONS

&

A QUILT

By Sue Akerman

The complete guide to making a beautiful quilt and cushions, with a profusion of floral crewel stitches, instructions and sketches, which can be utilized in many projects.

A book to inspire the needlewoman and enhance her creativity.

Published by

Triple T Publishing c.c.   Cape Town.

The upper six large blocks of Sarah-Jane's Quilt.

The lower six large blocks of Sarah-Jane's Quilt.

First published 1994
Second impression 1995
Triple T Publishing c.c.
29 Colenso Road
Claremont 7700.
Cape Town. South Africa.

ISBN 0-958-3873-1-1

Typesetting and reproduction by Fotoplate, Cape Town
Printed by Mills Litho, Cape Town
Photography: Lesley Turpin-Delport and Roger Wooldridge
Editing: Lesley Turpin-Delport

Copyright © Susan Akerman and Triple Publishing C.C.

All rights reserved. No part of this publication may be reproduced, stored in
a retrieval system or transmitted in any form or by any means. Use modern
equipment and technology (photocopiers) to enlarge or reduce the patterns
for your own personal use. Distribution or sale of any part of this book
infringes the laws of copyright.

AUTHOR'S ACKNOWLEDGEMENTS

While compiling this book there were numerous people who gave me
encouragement. To all of you I would like to say a very big thank you.
My sincere appreciation to Lesley Turpin-Delport and Geoff. Preston-
Thomas for their endless encouragement, belief in me, and hours spent
on editing and photography.
To my Mum and late Dad, who recognised at an early age, my need to
create, and encouraged me at every turn.
Special thanks to my students who gave of their precious time to help
with the embroidery on the quilt. In particular – Magda Lamb, Maureen
Heath, Linda Tedder, Veronica Henwood, Evette Ellison, Wendy Warr,
Lesley Warr, Wendy Lumley, Brenda Brawn and Marlene Turner.
Last, but most certainly not least, to my family. None of my work would
be possible without the love and support of my wonderful husband
Hugh, and my special children Gareth, Mark and Sarah-Jane. They have
gone without hours of my time and attention so that this book could be
completed.

CONTENTS

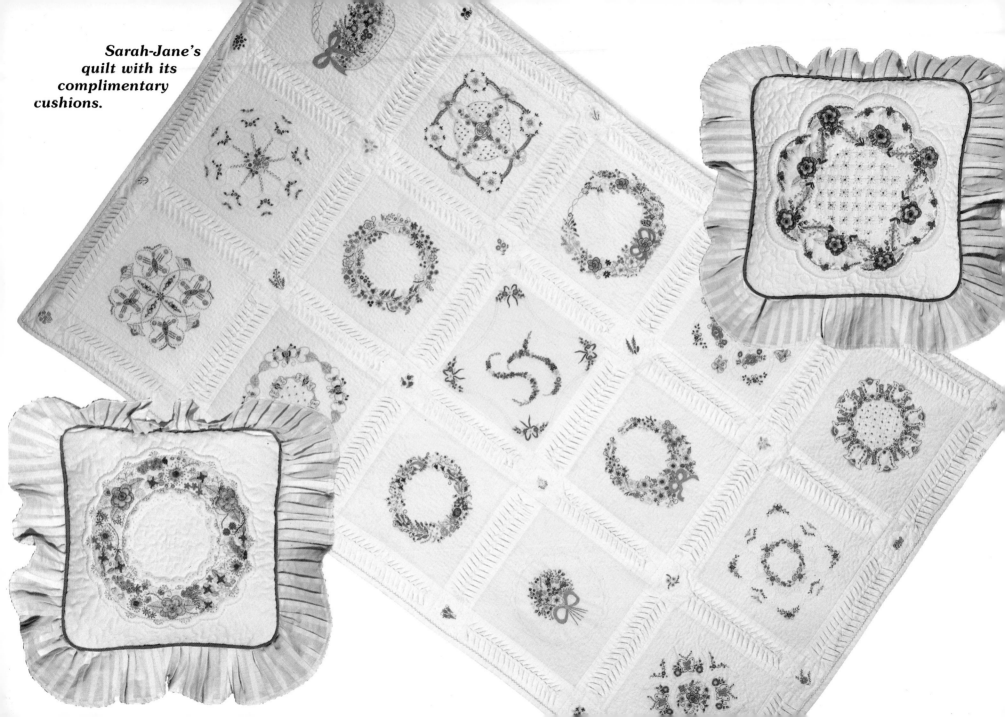

Sarah-Jane's quilt with its complimentary cushions.

INTRODUCTION

It is not surprising that my love for nature and flowers abounds, having grown up in the beautiful Natal Drakensburg. Memories of summer evenings, scent from the garden, hawk moths and butterflies filled the air.

You can imagine my delight when I discovered I could design flowers and little gardens with a needle and thread.

Teaching embroidery gives me great pleasure. The therapeutic value and enjoyment derived from putting thread and needle together to create is endless. It is almost an escape from the harsh realities of the world we live in.

Embroidery for me, has endless possibilities. Please feel free to use these patterns as they are, for cushions or quilts, or use parts of them to create your own features on collars, pockets, napkins, sweaters etc.

I hope that you have hours of enjoyment working with these patterns. I know that once you have started you will dream of having 48 hours in every day for embroidery.

My only wish is that I could see all your wonderful quilts and creations.

Happy creating

IN THE BEGINNING . . .

FABRICS

It is important to keep in mind that you are going to spend hours of work on your embroidery, making an heirloom. It is worth spending a little more money on a good fabric rather than spoiling your work by using an inferior one. Make sure the fabric you choose holds its shape. The quilt pictured in this book was made of seed cloth [loomstate cotton]. I love working on silk for smaller projects. The rich lustre of the silk enhances the embroidery. Natural fibres or fabrics with some texture tend to enhance your embroidery and add interest to your work.

SCISSORS

Scissors should be small and well sharpened.

HOOPS

An embroidery frame or hoop stops your work from puckering – especially when you are working intensely in some areas.
Embroidery hoops come in all shapes and sizes. Choose one that you find comfortable to work on.
When placing your fabric into your hoop be sure that the warp and the weft of the fabric run vertically and horizontally across your hoop.
At all times keep your fabric taut in your frame.

NEEDLES

Blunt nosed needles for weaving stitches.
Crewel needles, size 7 or 8 for most stitches.
Straw needles for bullion knots and cast-on buttonhole.
The size of the needle obviously varies according to the thickness of the thread or the number of strands that you are using.

THREADS

Embroidery can be done using almost any type of thread. I have used DMC stranded cottons throughout this quilt. Tremendous flexibility will be gained by varying the number of strands of thread in your needle. The more strands you use, the heavier looking the flower. The less strands you use, the finer the flower will be.

CHOOSING COLOURS

Many quilters are unsure of themselves when it comes to colour. So many people feel that they have no colour sense, and are quite terrified when asked to choose their own colours. Colour is a very personal thing. What one person likes, someone else is sure to dislike.
I am always happiest when my students choose their own colours as their work then becomes more individual and an extension of themselves. What joy when they find that the colours they have chosen have worked well together.
A good piece of advice; if at a loss in choosing colours, find a piece of fabric that you really love and build on it. Add one colour at a time until the range you require is complete.
Remember that in nature or in a garden, any colour seems to go with another. A bright red rose never seems out of place next to pink flowers in a garden setting. Do try unusual colours together as the effect may be just what you are looking for.
Ultimately what really counts is that you enjoy your work and are happy with it.

COLOURS USED IN THIS QUILT

DMC stranded cotton (15 colours)

Greens – 3363,523,471	Yellow – 725,745
Blues – 340,341,794,793	White
Pinks – 335,224,3722,760	Cream

WASHING AND CARE OF EMBROIDERED ITEMS

Use warm water and a mild washing soap. Soak and squeeze your work gently. Never wring the water out of your work. Dry flat and face down. Leave it until almost dry. Place your work face down on a towel, and using a moderately hot iron press your work carefully. You do not want to flatten your embroidery stitches by ironing over them.
When washing a quilt, put the quilt in a bathtub and apply the same rules as above. If your washing machine is big enough to fit your quilt comfortably, spin the excess water out of your quilt. If not, leave the excess water to drain out of the quilt while lying in the bath. Throw the quilt over the washline, face down. Do not expose the embroidery to unnecessary sunlight.
Do not iron your quilt once it has been quilted.

... THERE IS A QUILT

GETTING STARTED ON YOUR QUILT

Make yourself 3 templates out of thin plastic, cardboard, or old X-ray sheets.

Large blocks	Corner pieces/Baby blocks	Sashing
34 x 34cm	10 x 10cm	34 x 10cm

Be sure to be very accurate when drawing your templates. Having accurate templates will facilitate the easy sewing together of your quilt. Using the template, mark the squares that you are going to embroider.

When drawing around the template, with an Hb pencil, make a dark dot at each corner. This corner spot helps with the piecing when joining your sashings. Cut your fabric 1cm bigger all the way around. These pencil lines you have drawn around the template become your sewing lines when joining the pieces together.

Cut your muslin, the same size as your squares (large blocks page 43) and corner pieces (baby blocks page 33). Remember to add the 1cm seam allowance.

Transfer the embroidery patterns onto the fabric using an Hb pencil or dressmaker's carbon.

Tack the muslin to the back of the fabric to be embroidered.

Place the blocks into the hoop and complete the embroidery using the suggestions provided in the flower combinations (page 17) and stitch glossary (page 73).

Cut out the corner pieces (baby blocks) page 33, and embroider them.

Once all the embroidery is complete, you can think about joining the pieces together.

Make up the sashings as explained on page 10 – flat tucks.

Once the pieces have been joined you can prepare for quilting.

REQUIREMENTS FOR QUILTS

	SINGLE BED	QUEEN SIZE BED
Finished size	Width 142cm x length 230cm	Width 240cm x length 240cm
No. of blocks (large)	15	25
No. of corners (baby blocks)	24	36
No. of sashings	38	60

Fabric required 1.15 wide	6.30m/4.10m	11.25/7.25m
Muslin required 90cm wide	3.0m	4.75m
Backing required	work out according to the width of your fabric.	
Batting required	work out according to the width of your batting.	
Binding required	7.5m	± 10 m

The second figure, under fabrics required, is the amount needed if you do ordinary sashings and do not flat tuck them.

TRANSFERRING YOUR PATTERN ONTO FABRIC

LARGE BLOCKS

For a quilt you will have to put these patterns onto a grid or photocopy machine and enlarge them to fit your 34 x 34cm squares.

I use a soft lead pencil to transfer my patterns onto fabric. I worry about the long term effects of the chemical marking pens.

Place your fabric over your pattern, making sure that it is centred and that the warp and weft run horizontally and vertically to your pattern.

There are numerous ways to transfer a pattern onto fabric.

1. Place your pattern onto the light box. Centre the fabric over your pattern and using a soft pencil trace the design. I never fill in too much detail, but merely trace the outline of the flowers and leaves. You do not want to end up with a huge amount of pencil lines on the fabric.
2. A window, with good light behind it, works well. Using masking tape, tape your pattern to the window. Now centre your fabric square over this and masking tape it in position. Trace your pattern.
3. A glass table with a light underneath works in the same way as a light box.

Dark Fabrics

These always pose a problem. A light coloured dressmaker's carbon works well. Place the carbon between the fabric and the pattern and with a pencil, trace the design. The pressure from the pencil transfers the pattern onto the fabric below.

CORNER PIECES (Baby blocks)

Cut your corners 12 x 12cm. This includes your seam allowance of 1cm all the way around. Place the template onto the fabric and mark around it. This will be your sewing line. Draw your cameo in the centre. Tack the muslin to the back of each corner piece. Complete your embroidery and colonial knots.

QUILTING TECHNIQUES

TRAPUNTO

(As seen in the two cushions)

This is also called high-relief quilting and is an attractive form of quilting where selected areas of the design are padded to give a raised effect.
It is a painstaking and time consuming technique, but well worth the effort when the final effect is seen.
Prepare for *trapunto* quilting by sewing the top fabric and muslin together. The *trapunto* is done once the candlewicking and embroidery are complete. At the back of your work pry the weave of the muslin apart or make a slit in the back fabric or muslin. With a toothpick or sharp bodkin push small amounts of wadding into the area to be padded. If you have had to slit the back fabric then you will need to whip the slit together with a herringbone or whip stitch. Some of these designs lend themselves to trapunto. Pad the areas between 2 rows of colonial knots or some of the bigger flowers to give a special raised effect.

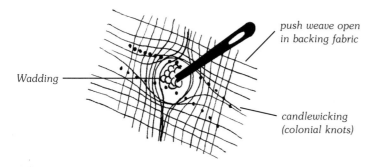

Wadding — push weave open in backing fabric — candlewicking (colonial knots)

TRADITIONAL QUILTING

(Preparing for quilting)

Basting The three layers required for quilting are the essence of the quilt. The stitches that travel through and secure the layers together define the design of the quilt. The "TEXTILE SANDWICH" is made up of a lining, wadding and the ground fabric. Before you begin quilting baste the three layers together; first the lining, wrong side up, then the batting and finally the ground fabric, right side up. Baste from the centre out towards each of the corners. Make sure that the basting lanes are not more than 2 to 3

fingers apart and radiate out towards the edges. End the basting at the outer edge with a quilting knot or a backstitch. An unorthodox method of basting is to pin the layers together with special brass safety pins. This is the method I have used on this quilt.
Make sure that your top and backing are well pressed and lying flat. Clear a space in a room with a tiled floor. Masking tape your backing to the floor so that it is secure and taut. Lay your batting onto the backing and then your embroidered top. Starting in the centre and using 1″ safety pins, pin the three layers together. I use my fist as a guide and place the safety pins about 10cm apart. Obviously try not to pin the quilt where you would be sewing a quilting line. Smooth the top fabric towards the outer edges as you are pinning. Pin the entire quilt and then remove the masking tape. Insert the prepared quilt into a hoop or frame and you are ready to begin quilting.

Textile Sandwich

— lining
— wadding
— top fabric
— tacking lines

HAND QUILTING

Thread a quilting needle with 30cm of quilting thread. I use a betweens No. 10.
Tie a knot in the end of your thread. From the top insert your needle through the top fabric and the batting, about 2.5cm from where you are about to commence quilting. Bring your needle back up at the starting point and pull through giving the thread a tug so that the knot passes through the fabric and lodges in the batting.
With your left hand underneath and your right hand on top, work small running stitches along the quilting lines. Stitches must be small and even. To end off, repeat the procedure for starting. Make a knot in the thread, pulling it through and lodging the knot in the batting. Exit the thread at the back and cut it off flush with the fabric.

MACHINE QUILTING

The quilt pictured in this book has been machine quilted. I have quilted along all the seam lines. For straight quilting set your machine stitch length on 3.

LAYOUT OF QUILT

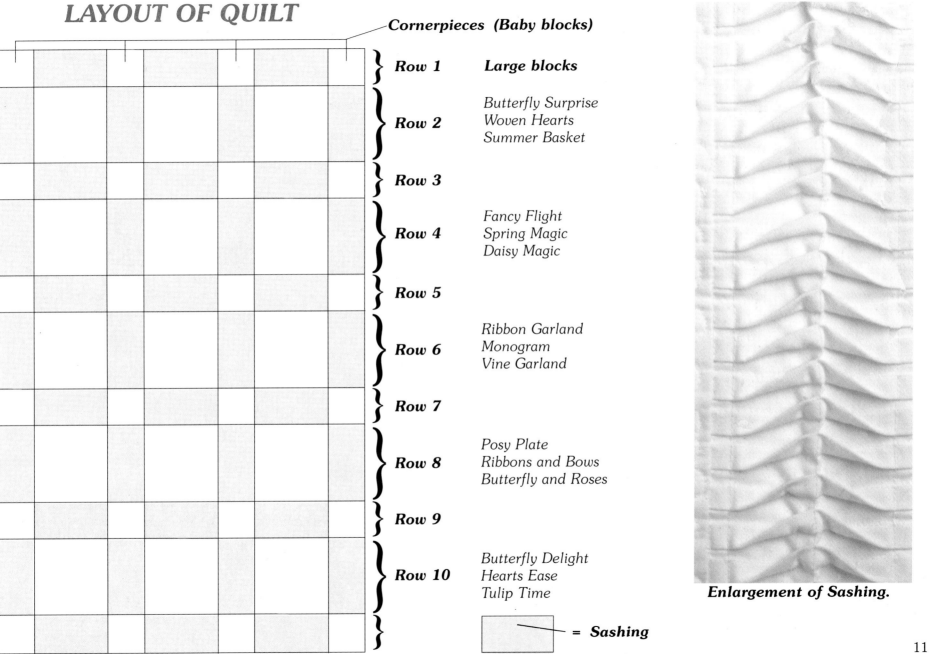

Cornerpieces (Baby blocks)

Row 1 — Large blocks

Row 2
Butterfly Surprise
Woven Hearts
Summer Basket

Row 3

Row 4
Fancy Flight
Spring Magic
Daisy Magic

Row 5

Row 6
Ribbon Garland
Monogram
Vine Garland

Row 7

Row 8
Posy Plate
Ribbons and Bows
Butterfly and Roses

Row 9

Row 10
Butterfly Delight
Hearts Ease
Tulip Time

= Sashing

Enlargement of Sashing.

11

I have a Bernina and use the walking foot for regular straight quilting. Use a good quality thread both on top and on your bobbin. To make the whole process easier and to avoid backache make sure that the quilt is well supported around your machine. I put my machine on a big table or pull up another table next to my machine cabinet. From either end roll the quilt up to the centre. Always sew your centre lines first. When starting pull the bobbin thread through to the top and sew 4 or 5 stitches on the same spot to anchor your sewing thread. Cut the loose threads off. Once you have sewn all the horizontal and vertical quilting lines you can commence with your "filler" quilting.

When doing this kind of quilting, always start in the centre.

On your machine, use the darning foot, good quality thread, and drop the feed dog. Put your machine at half speed. Start by bringing the bottom thread to the top and securing it with a few tiny stitches in the same spot. You are now in total control of your fabric. You need to take hold of your fabric with both hands in order to move it around at an even speed, thus creating an even stitch length. I create my own patterns as I work, wandering all over the fabric, filling spots that need to be filled and then moving on to new areas.

SASHINGS

Sashings should unify and contain a quilt. If you were to leave your sashings plain you would create a huge amount of negative space and a very uninteresting area. *Flat tucks* are used in Sarah-Jane's quilt.

Alternate Ideas:

Ruched Sashings:
Cut the sashing 75cm x 12cm and on both long sides sew a gathering thread. Gather your sashing up to fit your template. You now have a wonderful ruched effect.

Embroider a design onto the sashing.

Quilt a design onto the sashing.

Draw diagonal lines across the sashings and either couch or quilt these lines.

Pin tucks also create interest and can be sewn in various patterns. Embroidery can also be incorporated with them.

HOW TO MAKE FLAT TUCKS:

These tucks create wonderful light and dark values which enhance the embroidery. Take a piece of fabric 1.60m in length and half the width of the fabric. With a soft pencil mark lines across the width of your fabric every 3,5cm. These lines become your folding lines.
Set the position of your machine needle to the furthest position on the left. Fold your fabric along the first drawn line.
With the bulk of your fabric out to the left of your machine and the right hand edge of the machine foot on the fold of the fabric, sew a straight line across the width of the fabric.

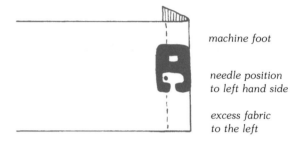

machine foot

needle position to left hand side

excess fabric to the left

Repeat the same process on each line that you have drawn.
Press your fabric, so that all the tucks lie in the same direction. Mark your sashings with the template {34cm x 10cm}. Be sure to leave a 1cm seam allowance the whole way around.
Cut out your sashings. . . (1cm bigger than the sewing or template lines).
Sew a straight line down the length of the sashing on either side to hold the tucks in place (approx. 1cm).

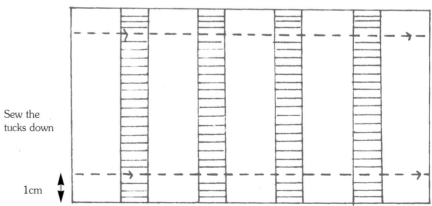

Sew the tucks down

1cm

Next draw a line up the centre of the sashing. From the opposite direction sew up the middle of your sashing on the drawn line. This makes the tucks stand up.

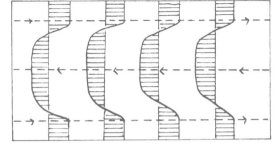

Sew up the centre in the opposite direction

JOINING THE BLOCKS AND SASHINGS TOGETHER

(How to assemble the Quilt top – See diagram page 11)

Lay all the blocks out on the floor to get an idea about where you are going to place them in the quilt. Make sure the colour is evenly balanced and that the tucks are all running in the same direction. When you are happy with your placement, check that your sewing template lines are clearly marked. Now you can begin joining your quilt. When joining, align the corner dots and pin them together, then pin along the sewing line between the dots. Join and sew your pieces one row at a time. Press all the seams to one side. Lastly sew the completed rows together, thus completing your quilt top.

COMPLETING THE EDGES

French Binding (Added binding)

The binding of a quilt should be strong; it should compliment the quilt top. There are many ways to sew bindings on and the one explained below is one that I find particularly successful.

Check the requirements table for the amount of binding that you are going to need. Cut 8cm strips of fabric on the straight grain of the fabric and join them all together, making sure that you have enough to go all the way around your quilt. With the wrong sides together fold the binding in half and iron it. You now have a 4cm double binding.

1. Once all the quilting has been completed, tack along the outside edges of the 'textile sandwich'. Leaving a 6mm ($\frac{1}{4}''$) seam allowance, trim the edges with scissors or a rotary cutter so that the edges of all three layers are even.

2. With right sides together, position the raw edge of the binding on the edge of the quilted top. Machine or hand stitch the binding to the quilt edge, approximately 6mm ($\frac{1}{4}''$) from the raw outer edge.

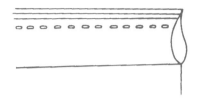

3. Fold the ironed edge to the back of the quilt and slip stitch it to the backing fabric over the stitching line.

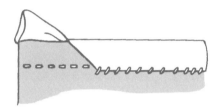

Turning the corner with French binding.

If the binding is very pliable, turn the corners and allow a natural mitre to form at the corner. The diagonal fold of this mitre can be secured with slip stitches. Complete all the corners in the same way. When you get back to the beginning again, join the two raw ends of the binding and cut off any excess binding. Now flip the binding over to the wrong side and with tiny slip stitches, sew it down. Decorate the binding with feather stitch in three strands of green embroidery floss.

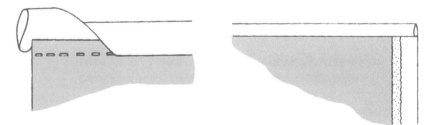

Alternatively, bind the two opposite sides of the quilt first. Then bind the other two sides catching in the binding on the first two sides to form a square corner, almost like a log cabin layout.

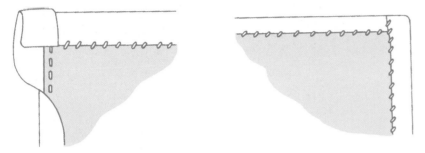

Square corner

If the quilt sides are straight but the corners are curved, piece a bias strip onto the straight binding so that the binding can follow the curve.
Clip the curve before rolling the bias over and slip stitching it to the back of the quilt.

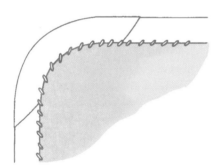

Use the designs from the quilt to create a collection of gorgeous scatter cushions.

SIT BACK AND ADMIRE YOUR MASTERPIECE!

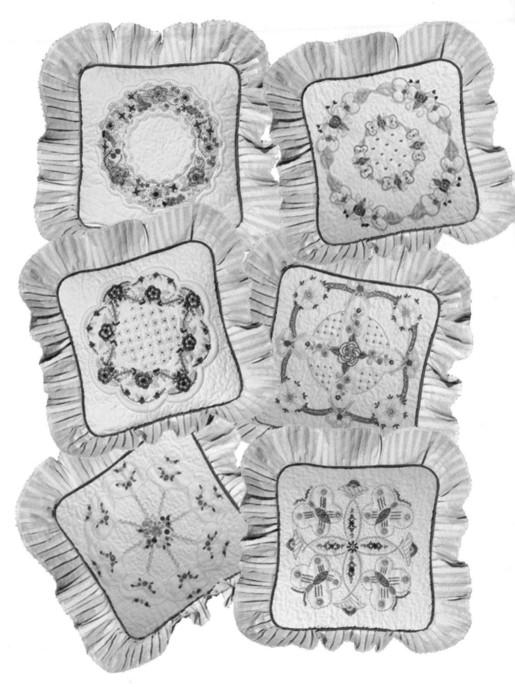

Evening Shadows.

...AND THEN TWO CUSHIONS

HOW TO MAKE UP A CUSHION

Step 1 Cut a piece of fabric 40cm x 40cm
Step 2 Trace the embroidery design onto the fabric.
Step 3 Tack the muslin to the back of your fabric.
Step 4 Complete the embroidery and trapunto.
Step 5 Make your 'textile sandwich' (refer illustration page 12). Tack well.
Step 6 Complete the quilting.

HOW TO ASSEMBLE THE CUSHION

Cushion Top

1. Round and clip the corners, so that the frills take the shape well and to facilitate sewing around the sharp corners.
2. Neaten the raw edges with a zig-zag or overlock stitch

Frill (pleated)

1. Cut a piece of fabric 12cm x 260cm in length.
2. Roll hem the one long side and overlock or zig-zag the other.
3. Make flat tucks across the width of the frill. (refer chapter page 10).
4. Join the two ends together forming a circle.
5. With right sides together, pin the frill to the cushion top. Always ease extra fabric in on the corners to allow for extra fullness.
6. Sew the frill to the cushion top.

If you would rather have a gathered frill, then the length of your frill should be twice the circumference of your cushion.

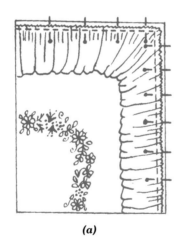

(a)

Back

1. Cut two pieces of fabric 25cm x 40cm. These two pieces overlap each other to form the back.
2. Finish off the raw edges with a zig-zag or overlock stitch.
3. On the 40cm side of each piece turn under 3cm. Press well and stitch. The two edges with the 'turn-under' lap over each other.
4. With the right sides together, pin the backs to the cushion top. Remember that the two pieces must overlap each other by 2cm in the centre.
5. Stitch the backs in place.
6. Turn the cushion inside out.
7. Purchase or make an inside cushion.

Buttons and buttonholes

For a truly old fashioned look, make handmade buttonholes and use mother of pearl buttons to finish it off perfectly.

(a) Pin the frill to the embroidered cushion top. Right sides together.

(b) Position the cushion backs over the embroidered top and frill, thus completing the cushion sandwich. Stitch in place.

(c) The completed cushion.

(b)

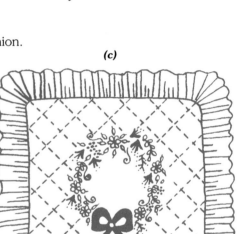

(c)

HANDY TIPS ON QUILTING AND EMBROIDERY

Always try to thread the end of your floss that has been pulled from the skein through your needle...the other end can be knotted.
To start, it is acceptable to use a neat knot or a tiny double stitch in the muslin.
To end off make 2 tiny backstitches in the muslin and thread the floss away and cut off.
If using one of the patterns for a framed piece or cushion make sure that you allow enough fabric around the design to suit the project.

Wash your hands before commencing your embroidery, and be sure to dry them well. Never apply hand cream to your hands before starting your work.
Do not lick the tip of the cotton when trying to thread it. If the cotton is damp you will find it hard to work with, especially when making bullion knots.
When making bullion knots be sure to keep the 'tail' of the thread short, and do not wrap the thread too tightly around the needle.

HAND EMBROIDERED FLOWER COMBINATIONS

I have only used fifteen colours in this quilt and have juggled them to suit each particular block. Choose colours to suit your personal taste.

These flowers have been created by combining simple crewel stitches to give the illusion of Hollyhocks, Daisies and Roses – a profusion of garden blooms. Be guided by the combinations shown but feel free to explore the potential in creating your own garden flowers. Add them into your own designs.

All stitches can be found in the Stitch Glossary.

In all these flower combinations I have made suggestions as to how many strands of cotton you should use for these flowers – if you wish to make smaller flowers work with less threads, for larger flowers work with more threads.

LAZY DAISY FLOWER
Petals
Work detached chain stitches in 2 strands of thread around the centre point.
I usually put in the first 4 chains (as illustrated) and then fill in-between.

Centre
Fill with French or Colonial knots
Use 3 strands of thread.

DANDELION
Using extended French knots work around the centre, spacing your knots evenly.
Use 2 or 3 strands of thread.

MIMOSA
Work the outside in single strand buttonhole. In a contrasting shade, fill the centre with tufting –
2 strands of thread.

GYPSOPHILA
Stem
Backstitch. Use 2 strands of thread.
Stab / straight stitch. Use 2 strands of thread.
Flowers
French Knots. Use No. 8 Candlewick thread or 3 strands of thread.

DAFFODIL
Stems
Stem stitch. Use 2 strands of thread.
Trumpet
Buttonhole. Use a single strand of thread.
Back Petals
Detached chain. Use 2 strands of thread.

THREE PETAL BUTTERFLY FLOWER
Butterfly
Work petals in a single strand of thread. Buttonhole stitch.
Stamens
Work in single strand extended french knots.

SWINGING BLOOMS
Work in cast-on buttonhole – each petal has 14 cast-ons. Use 3 strands of thread. Make 5 marks an equal distance apart around the outer perimeter of the flower. Come up in the centre and make your backstitch preparation from one of the outer marks to the centre. Cast on and pull through. Anchor your petal. When making your second petal do not come up in the centre, but in the 'crook' of your last petal [as illustrated]. Continue in the same way until your flower is complete. Make 5 petals.

PEKINESE FLOWER
Make 3 circles of tiny back stitch – use 2 strands. Starting on the outer row – work your pekinese stitch all the way around in a clockwise direction. The second row loops must overlap the back stitches of the outer row. Likewise the inner row. You can shade this flower quite successfully.
2 strands of a dark shade on the inner circle,
2 strands of a light shade on the outer circle and
1 of each on the middle circle.
Pack the centre with french or colonial knots in 3 strands of thread.

BABY PEEK

Make each circle with tiny backstitches using 2 strands of thread – now work your Pekinese on these. Fill centre with french or colonial knots.

WILD FLOWER

Stem

Coral stitch – 3 strands of thread.

Flower

Buttonhole. Use single strand of thread.
Do a double chain stitch to form an oval at the top of the flower. Use 3 strands.

SMALL BULLION DAISY

Leaves

Each leaf consists of two 8 twist bullion knots using 3 strands of thread.

Stems

Straight stitch using 2 strands of thread.

Flower

Each petal consists of two 8 twist bullion knots using 3 strands of thread.

FORGET ME KNOTS

French Knots. Use 3/6 strands (1 twist)
Make your centre first and then work 5 or 6 knots around the centre.

GRUB ROSE

Bullion Knots using 3/6 strands of thread
(11 twists throughout)
Centre – work 3 bullions side by side.
2nd row – work 4 bullions tightly around this centre, slightly overlapping.
3rd row – work 5/7 bullions around this.
The petals must overlap slightly, (as illustrated).

SWEET ROSE BUD

Centre – make a colonial knot using 6 strands of thread
1st row – working tightly around this knot, work 3 x 6 twist bullions – 3 strands of thread.
2nd row – this row is worked by doing 3 x 8 twist bullions around the previous row – 3 strands of thread.

OLD ENGLISH BUD

3 strands of thread throughout.

Centre

One 6 twist bullion knot

Outer Petals

2 x 8 twist bullions
When making a perfect bud, make your 6 twist bullion in the centre. Then working from one end of it to the other, make an 8 twist bullion on either side. Leaves 2 x 8 twist bullions – work these so that they either hug the bud or radiate out slightly. Use 3 strands of thread. For a slightly bigger bud work two 10 twist bullions around the bud before adding the leaves.

CREEPER

Stem

Coral stitch worked in 2 strands of thread.

Leaves

Cast-on buttonhole. To make these leaves 'loop', take a very small backstitch to start with. Cast on 18 times. Use 3 strands of thread.
To vary the size of the leaves, cast on varying numbers of stitches.

VINE TWIRL

Vine

Backstitch or stem stitch. Use 2 strands of thread.

Leaves

Extended chain stitch. Use 2 strands of thread.

LAZY DAISY FERN

Stem

Stem stitch. Use 2 strands of thread.

Leaves

Extended chain. Use 2 strands of thread.

FERNLEAF

Stem and leaves

Continuous extended flystitch. Use 2 strands of thread. Make one fly stitch after the other. Place a single strand French knot on the end of each frond.

WHEATEAR

See stitch glossary.

CYCLAMEN LEAF

Buttonhole stitch. Use a single strand of thread. Start at the left hand tip of the leaf and work around anticlockwise, perforating the centre, almost creating an 'anglaise' hole.

These details should help the needlewoman

Sweet rosebuds, lazy daisy fern, woven spider's web, whipped spider's web, looped bullion daisy and wild flower

Woven picot, old english rosebud, iris, agapanthus, looped bullion daisy and cyclamen leaves.

identify the different flower types.

Wisteria, grub rose, fuchsias, cast-on buttonhole daisy, bullion daisy and buttonhole pinwheel flower.

Winter flower, dandelion, shasta bullion daisy and cyclamen leaves.

WOVEN SPIDER'S WEB

See stitch glossary.
This can be worked in 2 shades. Start with dark thread and do two rows then change to a lighter shade. Use 3 strands of thread. This flower must have uneven spokes.

WHIPPED SPIDER'S WEB

See stitch glossary.
Use 3 strands of thread and work until all the spokes are covered.

IMPATIENS
Petals
Worked in single strand buttonhole.
The stitch between the petals is worked in cast-on buttonhole. 10 cast-ons using 3 strands of thread.
Centre
Fill with knots or leave empty.

BUTTONHOLE PIN WHEEL FLOWER

Work flower in buttonhole using a single strand of thread. Then make a row of french knots again using a single strand of thread all the way around.

WINTER FLOWER
Stem
Stem stitch. Use 1 or 2 strands of thread.
Leaves
Detached chain. Use 2 strands of thread.
Flowers
Each consist of 2 detached chains. Use 2 strands of thread.
Make a single strand French knot in a contrasting colour, at the tip of each chain.

FOXGLOVE

Leaves
Use fly or romanian stitch in single or double strand.

Stem
Backstitch using 2 strands of thread.

Buds
French Knots using 2 or 3 strands

Flowers
Buttonhole using a single strand.

Tip
Use a deeper shade for the buds. Shading the petals from dark at the top to light at the base can also be effective.

HOLLYHOCK

Leaves
Bullion knot using 3 strands of thread with 30 twists.

Flowers
Buttonhole. Single strand.

Buds
French knots using 3 strands of thread with 1 twist.

Leaves
Detached chain. Use 2 strands of thread.

LAVENDER

Leaves and Stem
Feather stitch. Single strand of thread.

Flower
Bullion knot. Use 2 strands of thread, 6 twists.

WISTERIA

Leaves
Make an 8 twist bullion using 3 strands of thread, and work a lazy daisy around it. Always start your lazy daisy at the point closest to the flower.

Flower
French knots or Colonial knots packed close together. Use 6 strands of thread.

AGAPANTHUS

Stem
Stem stitch. Use 2 strands of thread.

Flower
Extended fly stitch and straight stitch. Use a single strand of thread. Work your extended fly stitches evenly around the circle. With a deeper shade – make straight stitches in between the fly stitches.

FUCHSIA

Work in 3 strands of thread.

1. Lower petals. Make three 10 twist bullion knots.
2. On either side of these make a 13 twist bullion knot.
3. The top 3 petals are worked in cast-on buttonhole. Each petal consists of 2 cast-on buttonholes, each with 15 cast-ons. Use 3 strands of thread.
4. The stamens are extended French knots, worked in a single strand of thread.

LOOPED BULLION FLOWERS

The flower is worked in bullion knots, all with 20 twists in 3 strands of thread. Work the outer row first, then with a contrasting colour work the inner row. Making sure that your inner petals do not hide the outer row. [as illustrated]

Centre
Fill the centre with French knots in 3 strands of thread.

LOOPED BUD

Stem
Back stitch in 2 strands.

Flower
Bullion knot. Make the back loop first – 30 twist and 3 strands of thread.

Now make the front loop. A 25 twist bullion knot using 3 strands of thread. (See illustration for needle positions).

Calyx
12 twist bullion knot using 3 strands of thread. This must cover the base of the bud.

Stamens
Extended French knots. Use single strand of thread. Catch the bottom loop when coming up through the fabric to make your knot.

BUTTONHOLE BUD

Stem
Backstitch. Use 2 strands of thread.

Petals
2 petals, cast-on buttonhole, each consisting of 12 cast-ons in 2 or 3 strands of thread.

Stamens
Extended French knots. Use single strand of thread.

IRIS

Stem
Straight stitch. Use 3 strands of thread.

Lower petals
10 twist bullion knots. Use 3 or 6 strands of thread.

Top petals
12 twist, bullion knots. Use 3 or 6 strands of thread.

Centre
2 Colonial knots. Use 3 or 6 strands of thread.

BLOSSOM BUD

Petals
Double lazy daisy. Work in 2 shades of thread.

Stamens
Extended French knots. Use single strand of thread.

BULLION AND LAZY DAISY FLOWER

Leaves
8 twist bullion – lazy daisy around the bullion using 3 strands of thread. Can be done in 2 shades, the bullion in a lighter shade, the lazy daisy in a darker shade.

Stem
Straight stitch. Use 2 strands of thread.

Petals
Each Petal is made up of an 8 twist bullion with a lazy daisy around it. Come up in the centre to start making your lazy daisy.

BUTTONHOLE FLOWER

Work in buttonhole. Use 1 strand of thread.
Fill centre with French knots in 3 strands or tufting in 2 strands of thread.

KNOTTED FLOWER

The Outline
Work in colonial knots evenly spaced around the edge. Fill the centre with french knots using 3 strands of thread.

Stamens
Extended french knots single or 2 strands of thread.

SUNFLOWER

Centre
Work a whipped spider's web in 3 strands of thread.

Petals
Each petal consists of 2 cast-on buttonhole stitches each with 15 cast-ons and 3 strands of thread.

Stamens
Extended french knots using single strand of thread.

WOVEN PICOT FLOWER

Centre
Work a spider's web in 3 strands of thread. Pack with knots or fill with tufting. I have also used couching in some of the blocks.

Petals
Each have 3 straight stitches in 3 strands of thread. Starting in the centre, pack the rows of weaving tightly onto the straight stitches until they are completely covered.

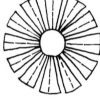

CABBAGE ROSE

Outer Petals
Work in single strand buttonhole. Then work a row of 20 twist bullion knots around the centre using 3 strands of thread, overlapping each one by half (see illustration). Pack the centre with knots using 3 strands of thread.

KNOTTED DAISY FLOWER

Centre
Using 2 strands of thread work a continuous chain. Start in the middle and circuit around until the centre is full.

Petals
Work in 2 strands of thread. Follow the notes on Bullion-Lazy Daisy combination.

LOOPY FLOWER

1. Make a 20 twist bullion. The starting and ending point of the bullion must be as close as possible. Use 3 or 6 strands of thread.
2. Work second 20 twist bullion as close as possible to the outside of the first bullion, the needle's ending point coming out in the centre of the first bullion.
3. Work the third bullion as close as possible to the first and second bulllions – the starting point of the next bullion is on the outer side of the first bullion, ending in the middle of the second bullion.
4. Single strand extended french knots are worked in between each petal. The 3 bullions should be interlocked and standing up.

This flower requires plenty of practice. Persevere, as it is well worth the effort once mastered.

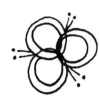

LEAVES
Work in romanian, fly or cretan stitch.
Use 1 or 2 strands of thread.

SHASTA BULLION DAISY
Work in 2 or 3 strands of thread.

Petals
6 twist bullion knots. Evenly space the bullions around the centre.

Centre
Pack with french knots or tufting. Use 2 or 3 strands of thread.

Step 1 *Step 2* *Step 3* *Step 4*

THE FLORAL ALPHABET

The A-Z in flowers on the following pages, are sketched full scale as seen in Sarah-Jane's quilt. These letters can be reduced to suit any project such as monograms or to illustrate a full name. Imagine the charm of an embroidered name, in one strand of thread, with delicately embroidered flowers.

The diagram for this block is shown on page 51.

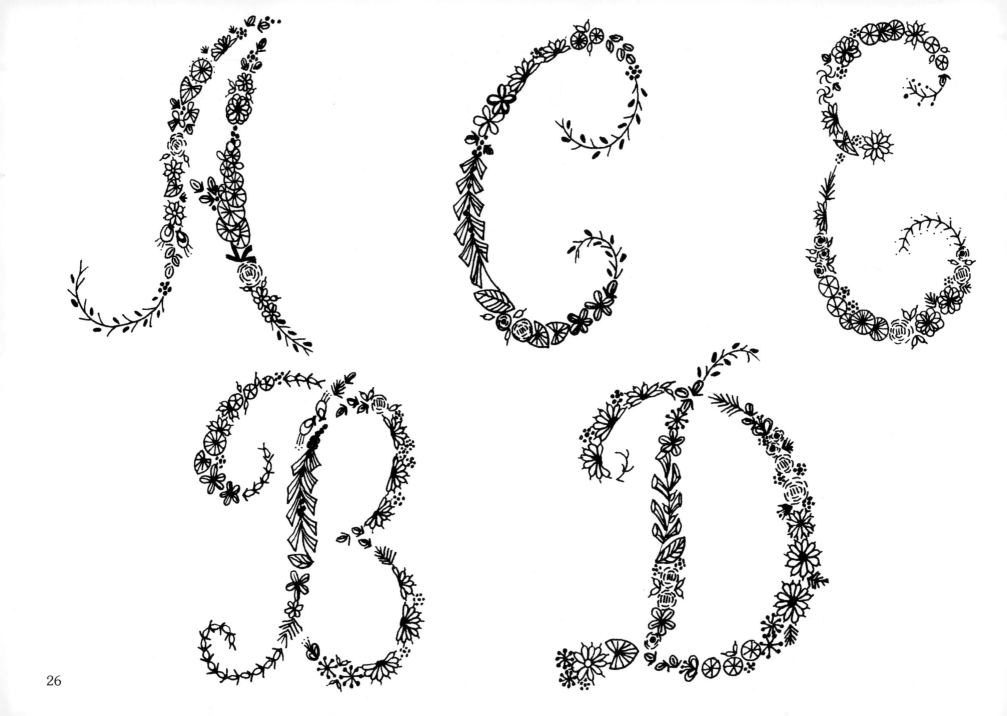

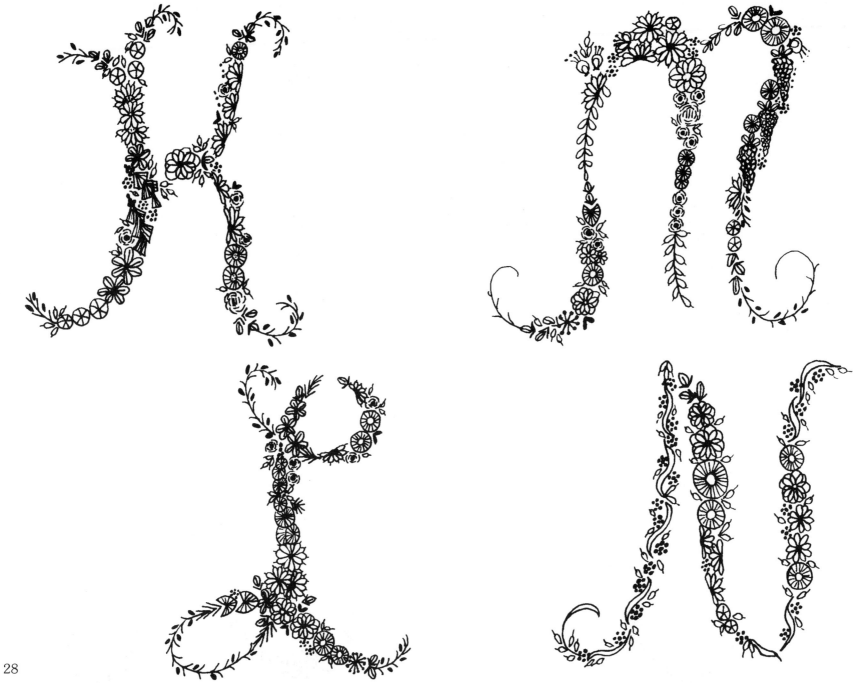

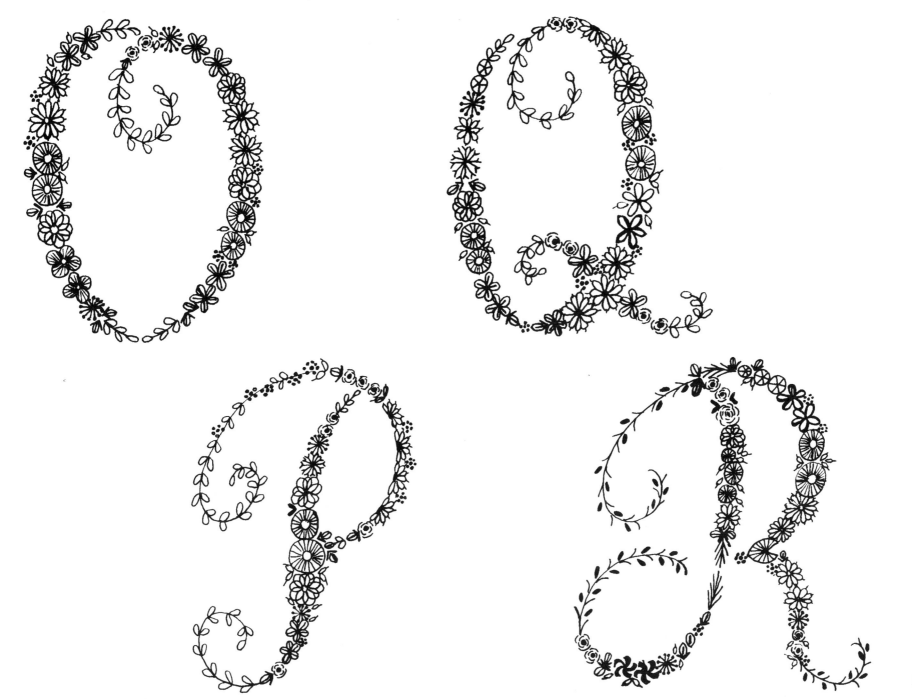

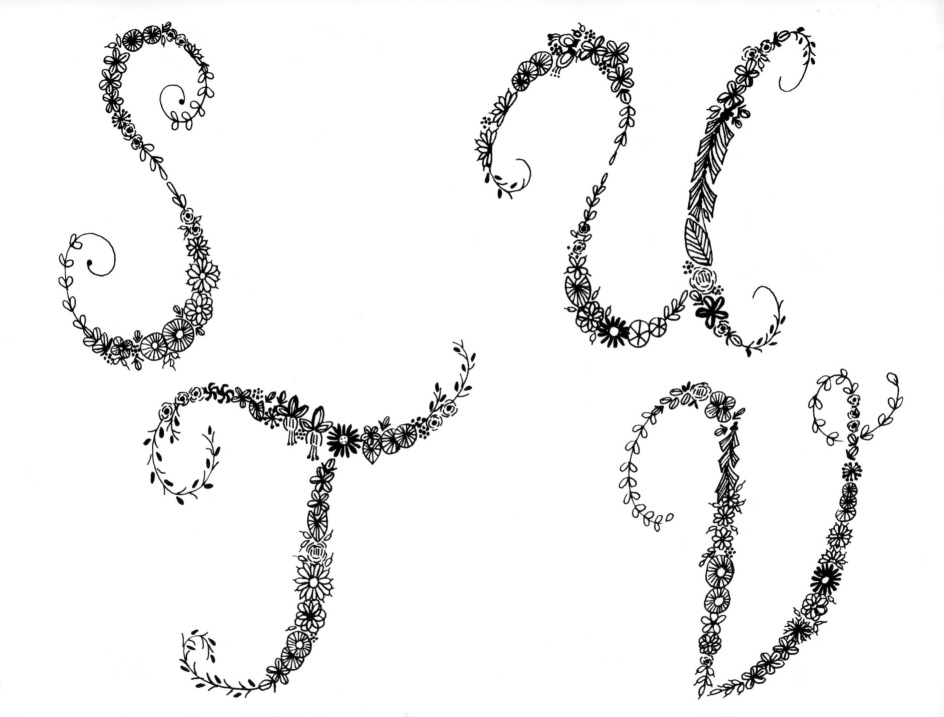

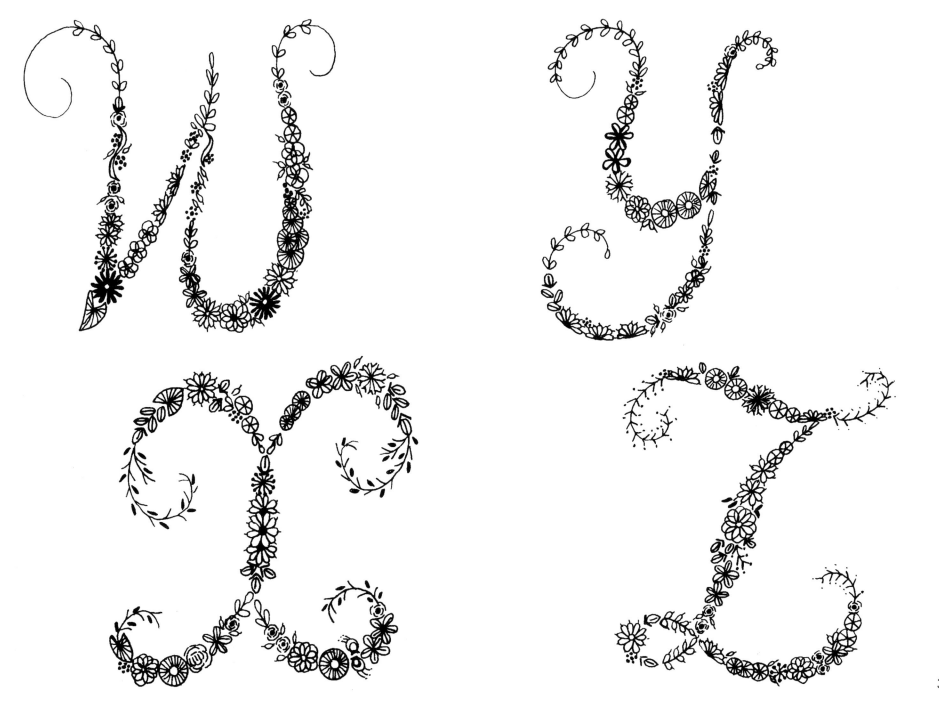

Hollyhock

The four baby blocks illustrated on this page are not incorporated in Sarah-Jane's quilt. Nor are sketches or drawings given for these four blocks.

They are shown to give the reader further ideas and stimulation to create her own flower stitches and individual corner pieces or baby blocks.

Three petal Butterfly flower

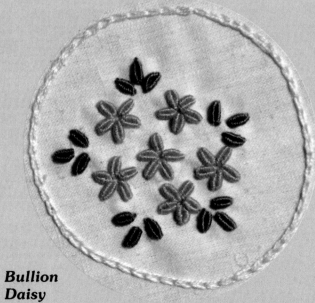

Bullion Daisy

Baby Peek

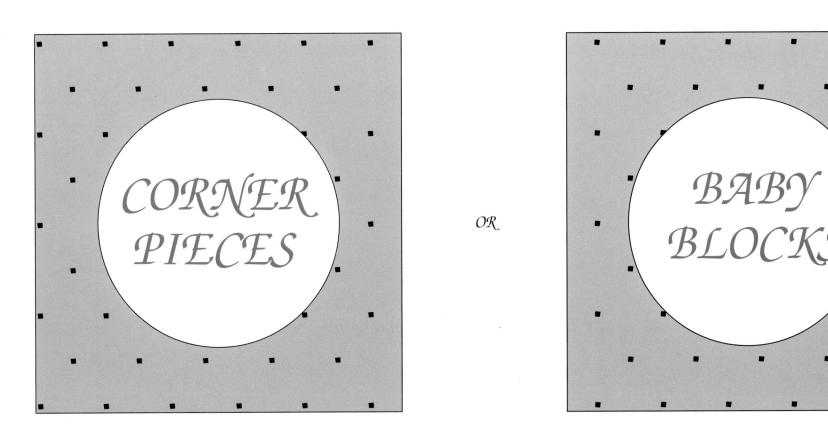

CORNER PIECES

OR

BABY BLOCKS

These blocks are the actual size of the instructions – use these sketches and select from the centre pieces on pages 36, 37, 40 and 41 or make up your own.

Wildflower

Dandelion

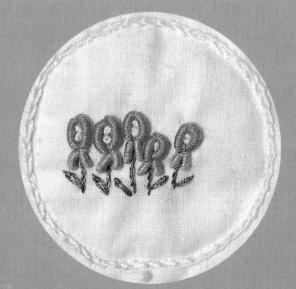

Iris

Agapanthus

Lavender

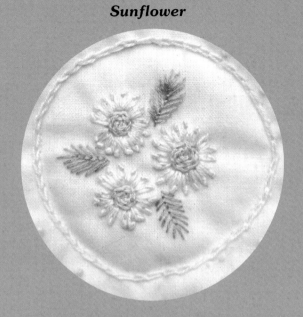

Woven Spider's Web

Bullion Lazy Daisy

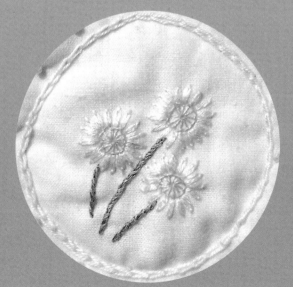

Lazy Daisy

Daffodils

Whipped Spider's Web

See page 34 for colour pictures of these corner pieces or baby blocks.

Wildflower

Buttonhole Pinwheel

Dandelion

Iris

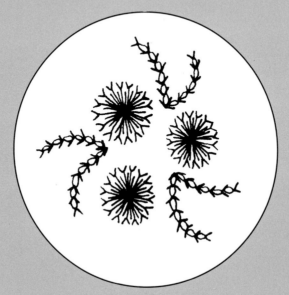

Agapanthus

Lavender

See page 35 for colour pictures of these corner pieces or baby blocks.

Woven Spider's Web

Bullion Lazy Daisy

Sunflower

Lazy Daisy

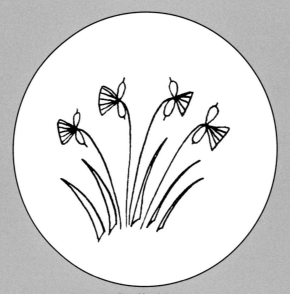

Daffodils

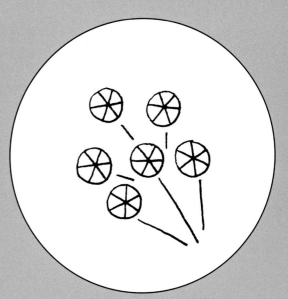

Whipped Spider's Web

Impatiens

Swinging blooms

Bullion Lazy Daisy

Foxgloves

Looped Bullion

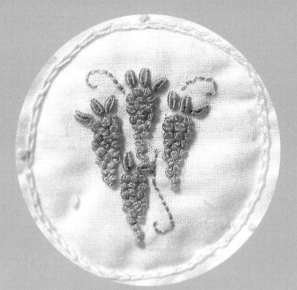

Wisteria

Woven Picot

Shasta Bullion Daisies

Fuchsias

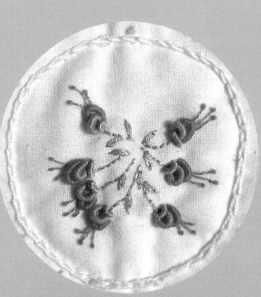

Looped Bullion Bud

Mimosa

39

See page 38 for colour pictures of these corner pieces or baby blocks.

Impatiens

Grub rose with old English buds

Swinging blooms

Bullion Lazy Daisy

Foxgloves

Looped Bullion

See page 39 for colour pictures of these corner pieces or baby blocks.

Wisteria

Woven Picot

Shasta Bullion Daisies

Fuchsias

Looped Bullion Bud

Mimosa

TWO CUSHIONS

The interesting rhythm created by quilting is clearly seen in these two designs. Notice how the *trapunto* gives a high relief effect while the *random background quilting* creates texture and movement within the design. The *pleated* frill also gives added dimension to the whole.

The drawings for these two cushions are on pages 42 and 52.

Circle of flowers

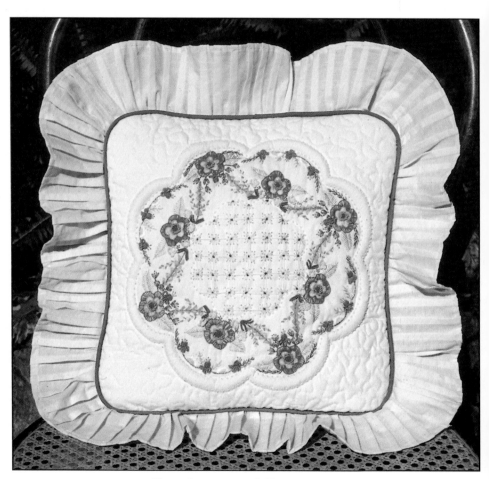

Foxgloves and Roses

LARGE BLOCKS

These garland designs lend themselves to a number of interpretations. Enlarged they would look striking on a continental pillow case, and reduced they would be enchanting as a pincushion or lavender bag.

The drawings for these two cushions are on pages 45 and 49.

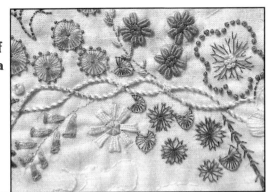

Vine Garland

Ribbon Garland

VINE GARLAND

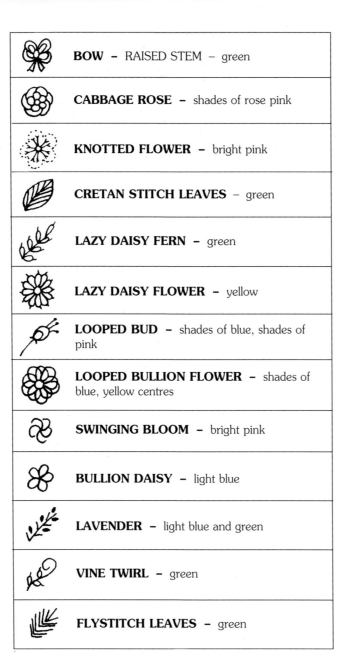

	BOW – RAISED STEM – green
	CABBAGE ROSE – shades of rose pink
	KNOTTED FLOWER – bright pink
	CRETAN STITCH LEAVES – green
	LAZY DAISY FERN – green
	LAZY DAISY FLOWER – yellow
	LOOPED BUD – shades of blue, shades of pink
	LOOPED BULLION FLOWER – shades of blue, yellow centres
	SWINGING BLOOM – bright pink
	BULLION DAISY – light blue
	LAVENDER – light blue and green
	VINE TWIRL – green
	FLYSTITCH LEAVES – green

 WISTERIA KNOTTED FLOWER – shades of blue
LEAVES – green

 KNOTTED FLOWER – yellow

 WHIPPED SPIDER'S WEB – blue

 OLD ENGLISH BUD – blue

 BUTTONHOLE FLOWER – yellow and blue with yellow centre

 SWEET ROSE BUD – shades of pink

 MIMOSA – shades of yellow

 AGAPANTHUS – blue

 GRUB ROSE – pink

 BUTTONHOLE PINWHEEL FLOWER – yellow

 SUNFLOWER – yellow

 GYPSOPHILA – white and green

 VINE – WHIPPED STEM STITCH cream and green

Flowers are loves truest language.
– Benjamin

VINE GARLAND

Colour photograph on page 43

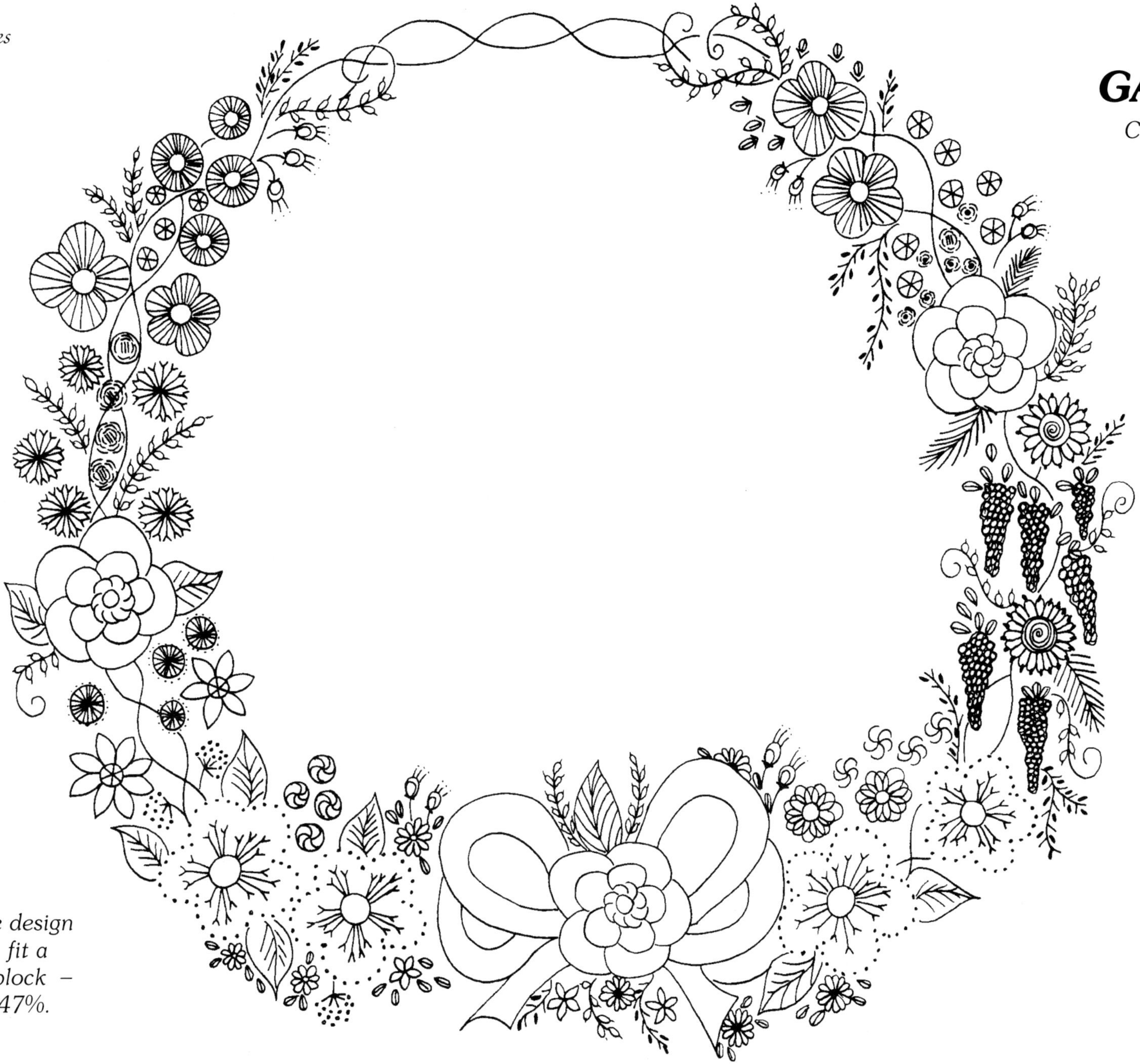

To make the design on this page fit a 34 x 34cm block – enlarge to 147%.

Butterfly Surprise

Woven Hearts

Summer Basket

Fancy Flight

Spring Magic

Daisy Magic

Posy Plate

Ribbons and Bows

Butterflies and Roses

Butterfly Delight

Hearts Ease

Tulip Time

47

RIBBON GARLAND

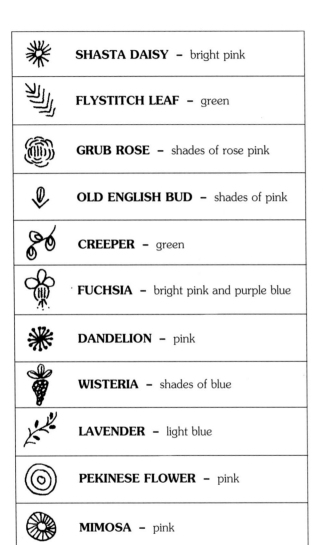

SHASTA DAISY – bright pink	
FLYSTITCH LEAF – green	
GRUB ROSE – shades of rose pink	
OLD ENGLISH BUD – shades of pink	
CREEPER – green	
FUCHSIA – bright pink and purple blue	
DANDELION – pink	
WISTERIA – shades of blue	
LAVENDER – light blue	
PEKINESE FLOWER – pink	
MIMOSA – pink	

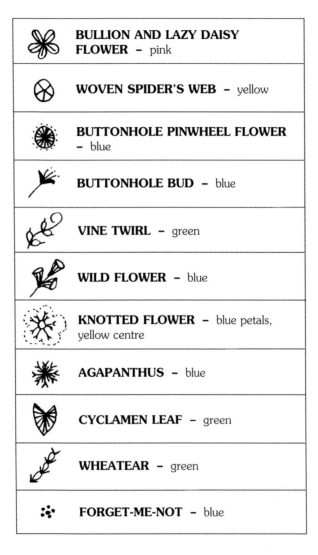

BULLION AND LAZY DAISY FLOWER – pink	
WOVEN SPIDER'S WEB – yellow	
BUTTONHOLE PINWHEEL FLOWER – blue	
BUTTONHOLE BUD – blue	
VINE TWIRL – green	
WILD FLOWER – blue	
KNOTTED FLOWER – blue petals, yellow centre	
AGAPANTHUS – blue	
CYCLAMEN LEAF – green	
WHEATEAR – green	
FORGET-ME-NOT – blue	

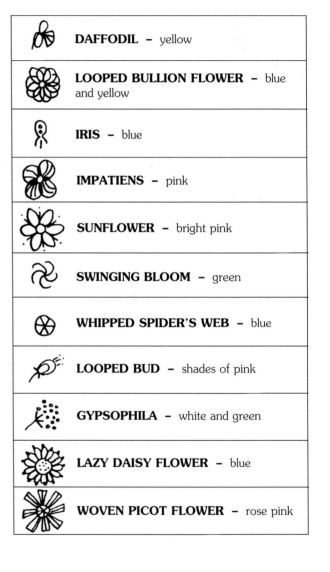

DAFFODIL – yellow	
LOOPED BULLION FLOWER – blue and yellow	
IRIS – blue	
IMPATIENS – pink	
SUNFLOWER – bright pink	
SWINGING BLOOM – green	
WHIPPED SPIDER'S WEB – blue	
LOOPED BUD – shades of pink	
GYPSOPHILA – white and green	
LAZY DAISY FLOWER – blue	
WOVEN PICOT FLOWER – rose pink	

More than anything I must have flowers, always, always.
— Monet

RIBBON GARLAND

Colour photograph on page 43

To make the design on this page fit a 34 x 34cm block — enlarge to 143%.

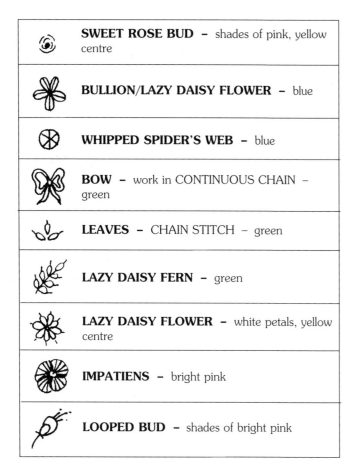

SWEET ROSE BUD – shades of pink, yellow centre

BULLION/LAZY DAISY FLOWER – blue

WHIPPED SPIDER'S WEB – blue

BOW – work in CONTINUOUS CHAIN – green

LEAVES – CHAIN STITCH – green

LAZY DAISY FERN – green

LAZY DAISY FLOWER – white petals, yellow centre

IMPATIENS – bright pink

LOOPED BUD – shades of bright pink

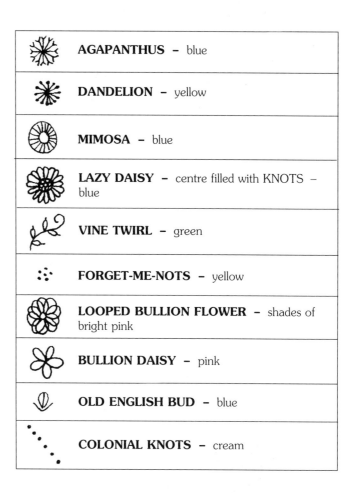

AGAPANTHUS – blue

DANDELION – yellow

MIMOSA – blue

LAZY DAISY – centre filled with KNOTS – blue

VINE TWIRL – green

FORGET-ME-NOTS – yellow

LOOPED BULLION FLOWER – shades of bright pink

BULLION DAISY – pink

OLD ENGLISH BUD – blue

COLONIAL KNOTS – cream

The flowers are nature's jewels,
with whose wealth
she decks her summer beauty.
– Anonymous

S-J
MONOGRAM

Colour photograph
on page 25

To make the design on this
page fit a 34 x 34cm block
– enlarge to 154%.

CIRCLE OF FLOWERS

 COLONIAL KNOTS – cream
WHIPPED STEM STITCH – cream and green

 EXTENDED FRENCH KNOTS – cream and blue

 CABBAGE ROSE – shades of rose pink

 KNOTTED FLOWER with circle of DETACHED CHAIN around the centre – pink

 IMPATIENS – shades of blue

 HOLLYHOCK – bright pink

 GRUB ROSE – blue

 LOOPED BULLION FLOWER – shades of yellow

 BULLION AND LAZY DAISY FLOWER – yellow

 WHEATEAR – green

 OLD ENGLISH BUD – blue

 FLY STITCH LEAF – green

 GYPSOPHILA – white and green

 LOOPY FLOWER – yellow

 WHIPPED SPIDER'S WEB – blue

 VINE TWIRL – green

 BABY PEEK FLOWER – blue

 BULLION DAISY – blue

 LAVENDER – blue and green

 SHASTA DAISY – with WHIPPED SPIDER'S WEB in centre – yellow

 CYCLAMEN LEAF – green

 SWEET ROSE BUD – blue

*The amen of nature
is always a flower.
– Holmes*

*As seen on the cushion
on page 42*

*To make the design on
this page fit a 34 x 34cm
block – enlarge to 151%.*

FOXGLOVES AND ROSES

*As seen on the cushion
on page 42*

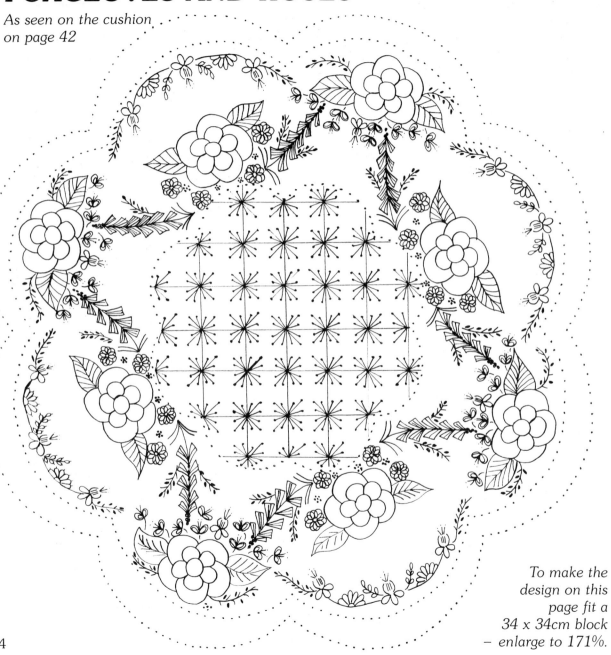

*To make the
design on this
page fit a
34 x 34cm block
– enlarge to 171%.*

CABBAGE ROSE – shades of rose pink

FOXGLOVE – bright pink

FLYSTITCH LEAF – green

FUCHSIA – pink and blue

LAZY DAISY FERN – green

LAVENDER – blue and green

LOOPED BULLION FLOWER – yellow

BLOSSOM BUD – blue

FORGET-ME-NOT – blue

CENTRE GRID
EXTENDED FRENCH KNOTS – light blue

COUCHING – cream and green

COLONIAL KNOTS – cream around the
basic design

BUTTERFLY SURPRISE

To make the design on this page fit a 34 x 34cm block – enlarge to 149%.

Colour photograph on page 46

FOUR OUTER FLOWERS
BASE – WHIPPED STEM STITCH – cream/green.
CENTRE – fill with FRENCH KNOTS – yellow.
PETALS – CHAIN STITCH with EXTENDED FRENCH KNOTS in between – blue.

CENTRE FLOWER – centre – SPIDER'S WEB – yellow.
PETALS – WOVEN PICOT – rose pink

WOVEN PICOT – rose pink with yellow centre

SWEET ROSE BUD – bright pink with yellow centre

DETACHED CHAIN LEAVES – green

SPIDER'S WEB – centre – SPIDER'S WEB – yellow.
PETALS – LAZY DAISY – yellow

WOVEN CHAIN – pink and blue

FEATHER STITCH – green

FORGET-ME-NOTS – blue

BUTTONHOLE PINWHEEL FLOWER – blue

LOOPED BUD – shades of pink

COLONIAL KNOTS – green and cream alternating

BUTTERFLY HEAD – fill the centre with FRENCH KNOTS – blue. Surround in CHAIN STITCH – pink

BUTTERFLY BODY – BUTTONHOLE PINWHEELS surrounded by FRENCH KNOTS – blue/pink/yellow/green

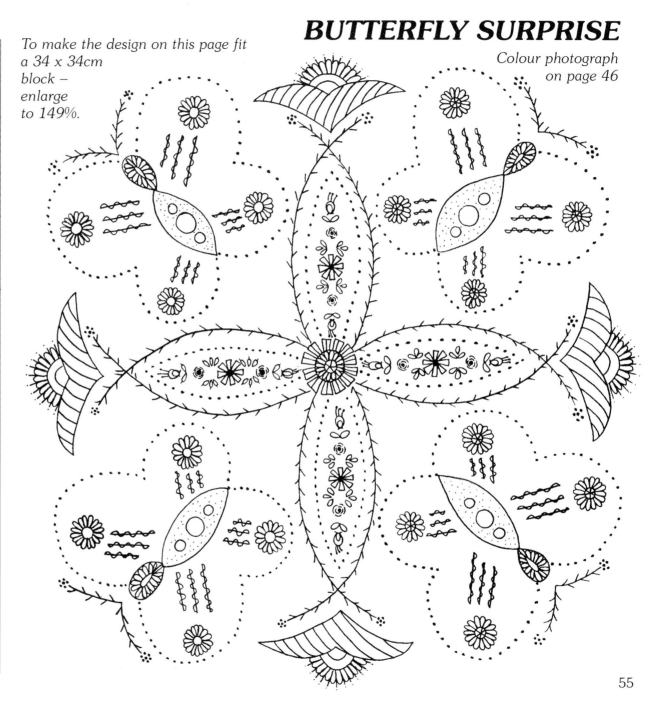

WOVEN
HEARTS

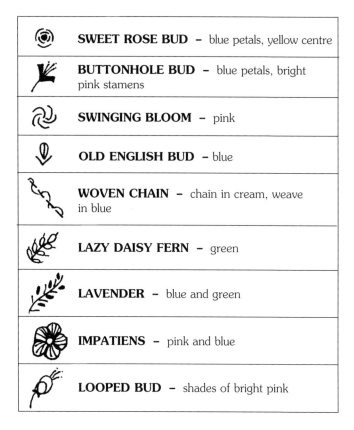

	SWEET ROSE BUD – blue petals, yellow centre
	BUTTONHOLE BUD – blue petals, bright pink stamens
	SWINGING BLOOM – pink
	OLD ENGLISH BUD – blue
	WOVEN CHAIN – chain in cream, weave in blue
	LAZY DAISY FERN – green
	LAVENDER – blue and green
	IMPATIENS – pink and blue
	LOOPED BUD – shades of bright pink

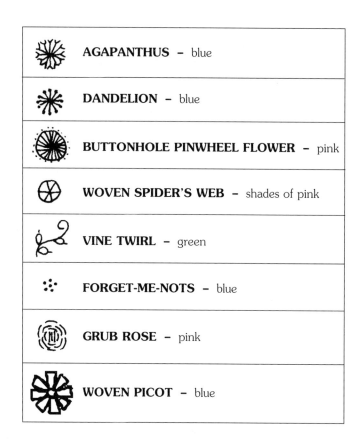

	AGAPANTHUS – blue
	DANDELION – blue
	BUTTONHOLE PINWHEEL FLOWER – pink
	WOVEN SPIDER'S WEB – shades of pink
	VINE TWIRL – green
	FORGET-ME-NOTS – blue
	GRUB ROSE – pink
	WOVEN PICOT – blue

To make the design on this page fit a 34 x 34cm block – enlarge to 164%.

SUMMER BASKET

 BOW – CONTINUOUS CHAIN and SATIN STITCH – blue

 BASKET
HANDLE – WHIPPED CHAIN – green and cream.
RIM – CHAIN – cream alternate bands (3 rows horizontal, 3 vertical).
BASE – WHIPPED CHAIN and COUCHING –

 WOVEN PICOT FLOWERS – rose pink

 IMPATIENS – blue with tufted centres

 SHASTA DAISY – bright pink with yellow centres

 SWEET ROSE BUD – pale pink

 KNOTTED DAISY FLOWER VARIATION – blue – fill centre with KNOTS – yellow

 LARGE LOOPED BULLION FLOWER – shades of pink with yellow centres

 ROMANIAN LEAVES – green

 BABY PEEK FLOWER – bright pink

 LAZY DAISY FERN – green

 WILD FLOWER – rose pink

 SMALL BULLION DAISY – blue

 LAZY DAISY FLOWER – dark blue

 BULLION AND LAZY DAISY FLOWER – blue

 SWINGING BLOOM – dark rose pink

 WHEATEAR – green

 LAZY DAISY FERN – green

 WHIPPED SPIDER'S WEB – blue and white

 LOOPED BUD – pink

 BUTTONHOLE BUD – pink

 FLYSTITCH LEAF – green

 AGAPANTHUS – blue

 BASE OF BASKET – FLY STITCHES at intersections – cream and blue

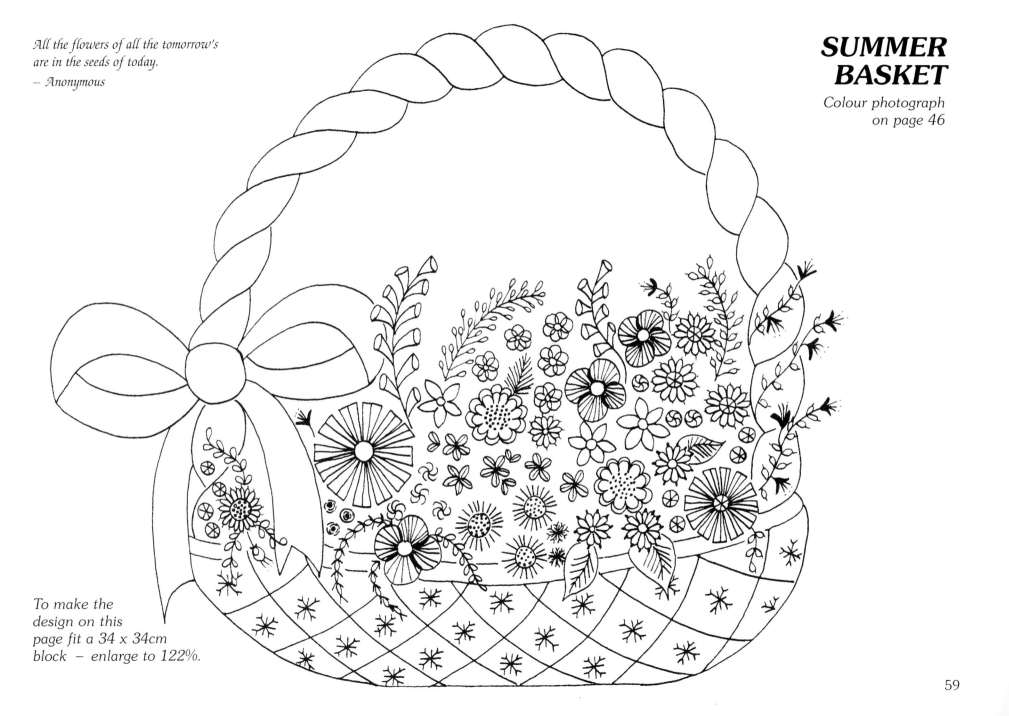

All the flowers of all the tomorrow's are in the seeds of today.
– Anonymous

SUMMER BASKET

Colour photograph on page 46

To make the design on this page fit a 34 x 34cm block – enlarge to 122%.

FANCY FLIGHT

Colour photograph on page 46

To make the design on this page fit a 34 x 34cm block – enlarge to 154%.

	ROMANIAN LEAVES – green
	THREE PETAL BULLION FLOWER – shades of blue
	VINE TWIRL – green
	BULLION DAISY – white and yellow
	EXTENDED FLY STITCH – green
	MIMOSA – bright pink petals, yellow centre
	BUTTONHOLE BUD – dark pink, dark green
	FORGET-ME-NOTS – yellow and cream/bright pink
	COUCHING – cream
	EXTENDED FRENCH KNOTS – yellow
	FRENCH KNOTS – pack the whole area – blue
	STEM STITCH – bright pink/blue
	BUTTONHOLE PINWHEEL FLOWER – bright pink

COLONIAL KNOTS – cream, pink

COUCHING – work buds at intersections – cream, blue

LARGE DAISIES
OUTLINE – COLONIAL KNOTS cream.
CENTRE – WHIPPED SPIDER'S WEB yellow.
PETALS – CHAIN STITCH with EXTENDED FRENCH KNOTS in between – blue.
LEAVES – BULLION KNOTS green

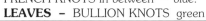

LAZY DAISY FLOWER VARIATION – work a WHIPPED SPIDER'S WEB in the centre –

MIMOSA – yellow

GRUB ROSE – shades of pink

BUTTONHOLE PINWHEEL FLOWER – bright pink/blue

SWEET ROSE BUD – shades of pink

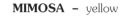

WHIPPED STEM STITCH – with knots in centre – shades of bright and light pink and yellow

BOW – COLONIAL KNOTS – pink.

OUTLINE – STEM STITCH – bright and light pink
FLOWERS – HALF LAZY DAISY – pack KNOTS in between – green, white, yellow

FLY STITCH LEAVES – green

LAVENDER – blue and green

To make the design on this page fit a 34 x 34cm block – enlarge to 160%.

DAISY MAGIC
Colour photograph on page 46

SPRING MAGIC

 CYCLAMEN LEAF – green

 OLD ENGLISH BUD – cream and pink

 ROMANIAN LEAF – green

 GRUB ROSE – shades of pink and cream

 FUCHSIA – bright pink and purple blue

 CREEPER – green

 LAVENDER – light blue and green

 FORGET-ME-NOTS – deep blue

 AGAPANTHUS – light blue and cream

 BUTTONHOLE PINWHEEL FLOWER – yellow petals with tufted yellow centre

 LOOPED BUD – shades of pink and blue

 WISTERIA – shades of blue
LEAVES – green

 VINE TWIRL – green

 BUTTERFLY BODY – pack with KNOTS – rose pink.
OUTLINE – STEM STITCH – bright pink.
WINGS – BUTTONHOLE – pink.
FEELERS – EXTENDED FRENCH KNOTS pink

 FOXGLOVE – shades of pink

 WHEATEAR – green

 KNOTTED DAISY FLOWER – blue petals, yellow centre

 DAFFODILS – yellow

 FLYSTITCH LEAF – green

 PEKINESE FLOWER – shades of pink

 WINTER FLOWER – green and white

 LOOPED BULLION FLOWER – shades of rose pink

 LADYBIRD – work in KNOTS – yellow and dark pink

 HOLLYHOCK – pale pink

 LAZY DAISY FLOWER – yellow

 SUNFLOWER – yellow and pink

Earth laughs in flowers.
— Emerson

SPRING MAGIC

Colour photograph on
page 46

To make the design on
this page fit a 34 x 34cm
block — enlarge to 128%.

POSY PLATE

 GRUB ROSE – shades of rose pink

 IMPATIENS – shades of pink

 LAZY DAISY FLOWER – with WHIPPED SPIDER'S WEB centre – pink petals, yellow centre

 BUTTONHOLE PINWHEEL FLOWER – blue and blue tufted centre

 LOOPY FLOWER – flower – shades of pink; centre – yellow

 BULLION DAISY – rose pink

 BULLION AND LAZY DAISY FLOWER – pale pink

 SWEET ROSE BUD – blue

 WOVEN SPIDER'S WEB – shades of blue, pink

 SWINGING BLOOMS – pink

 VINE TWIRL – green

 DANDELION – yellow

 LOOPED BUD – shades of blue

 OLD ENGLISH BUD – shades of blue

 CREEPER – CAST-ON BUTTONHOLE LOOPS – green

 IRIS – shades of pink

 GYPSOPHILA – white and green

 LAVENDER – blue and green

 KNOTTED FLOWER VARIATION with woven centre – rose pink

 BOW – RAISED STEM STITCH – light blue

 STEMS – WHIPPED CHAIN – green

 PLATE OUTLINE – EXTENDED FRENCH KNOT, COLONIAL KNOT, WHIPPED STEM STITCH – cream

Many flowers of love
Around thee be twined
and the sunshine of peace
shed it's joy or'e thy mind.
– Anonymous

POSY PLATE

Colour photograph on page 47

To make the design on this page fit a 34 x 34cm block – enlarge to 152%.

RIBBONS AND BOWS

 BOWS – CONTINUOUS CHAIN – green

 KNOTTED FLOWER – rose pink/blue

 WOVEN PICOT FLOWER – shades of pink

 BUTTONHOLE FLOWER – shades of yellow

 FLY STITCH LEAF – green

 VINE TWIRL – green

 BULLION DAISY – blue

 GYPSOPHILA – cream, green

 LAVENDER – blue and green

 RIBBON – work in WHIPPED CHAIN – cream and green (alternate)

 LOOPED BULLION FLOWER – bright pink

 FORGET-ME-NOTS – bright pink

 KNOTTED DAISY FLOWER VARIATION – bright pink. Fill the centre with KNOTS – yellow

 BUTTONHOLE PINWHEEL FLOWER – blue

 WHIPPED SPIDER'S WEB – rose pinks

 LOOPED BUD – blue/bright pinks

 LAZY DAISY FLOWER – blue

 SWEET ROSE BUD – blue

 WHEATEAR – green

*The pinks along my garden walks
have all shot forth
their summer stalks, thronging
their buds, 'mong tulips
hot, and blue forget-me-not.*

– Bridges

RIBBONS
AND BOWS

Colour photograph
on page 47

To make the design on
this page fit a 34 x 34cm
block – enlarge to 143%.

BUTTERFLY DELIGHT

BUTTERFLY
OUTLINE – STEM STITCH – blue
BODY AND HEAD – fill with kNOTS – blue
WINGS – work in BUTTONHOLE – blue

FERN LEAF – green with blue and bright pink flowers

VINE TWIRL – green

LOOPED BUD – blue/bright pink

LOOPED BULLION FLOWER – two tone bright pink

LAVENDER – green and blue

GRUB ROSE – blue

SWEET ROSE BUD – shades of pink

ROMANIAN LEAF – green

LAZY DAISY FLOWER – pink

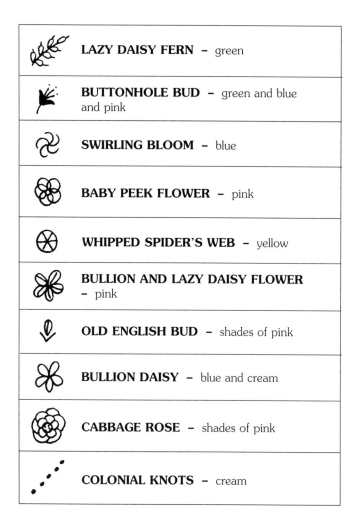
LAZY DAISY FERN – green

BUTTONHOLE BUD – green and blue and pink

SWIRLING BLOOM – blue

BABY PEEK FLOWER – pink

WHIPPED SPIDER'S WEB – yellow

BULLION AND LAZY DAISY FLOWER – pink

OLD ENGLISH BUD – shades of pink

BULLION DAISY – blue and cream

CABBAGE ROSE – shades of pink

COLONIAL KNOTS – cream

A 'thing' created is loved
before it exists.
– Chesterton

BUTTERFLY DELIGHT

*Colour photograph
on page 47*

*To make the design on
this page fit a 34 x 34cm
block – enlarge to 143%.*

BUTTERFLIES AND ROSES

Colour photograph on page 47

To make the design on this page fit a 34 x 34cm block – enlarge to 171%.

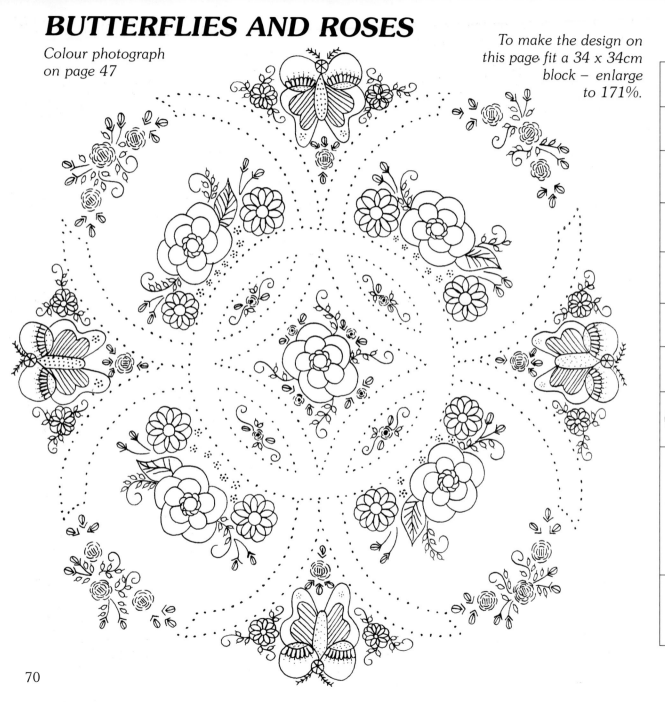

 SWEET ROSE BUD – yellow centre, deep rose petals

 FORGET-ME-NOTS – blue with yellow centre, bright pink/blue petals

 LOOPED BULLION FLOWER – shades of blue, yellow centre

 GRUB ROSE – shades of pink

 VINE TWIRL – green

 OLD ENGLISH BUD – shades of rose pink/blue

 FLY STITCH LEAF – green

 CABBAGE ROSE – shades of bright pink

 BUTTERFLY FEELERS – work in FLY STITCH – green
HEAD – work in WHIPPED SPIDER'S WEB – blue
OUTLINE – work in STEM STITCH – blue
UPPER WINGS – fill with KNOTS, LAZY DAISY and EXTENDED FRENCH KNOTS – yellow and pink

 BODY – fill with KNOTS – yellow
OUTLINE – work in STEM STITCH – blue
LOWER WINGS – work in BUTTONHOLE and FORGET-ME-NOTS – yellow and blue

To make the design on this page fit a 34 x 34cm block – enlarge to 138%.

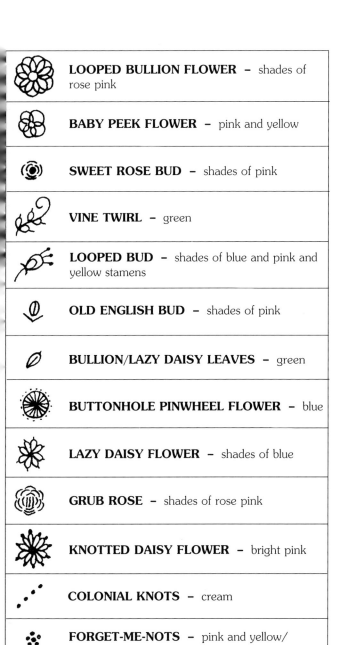

	LOOPED BULLION FLOWER – shades of rose pink
	BABY PEEK FLOWER – pink and yellow
	SWEET ROSE BUD – shades of pink
	VINE TWIRL – green
	LOOPED BUD – shades of blue and pink and yellow stamens
	OLD ENGLISH BUD – shades of pink
	BULLION/LAZY DAISY LEAVES – green
	BUTTONHOLE PINWHEEL FLOWER – blue
	LAZY DAISY FLOWER – shades of blue
	GRUB ROSE – shades of rose pink
	KNOTTED DAISY FLOWER – bright pink
	COLONIAL KNOTS – cream
	FORGET-ME-NOTS – pink and yellow/ blue and yellow

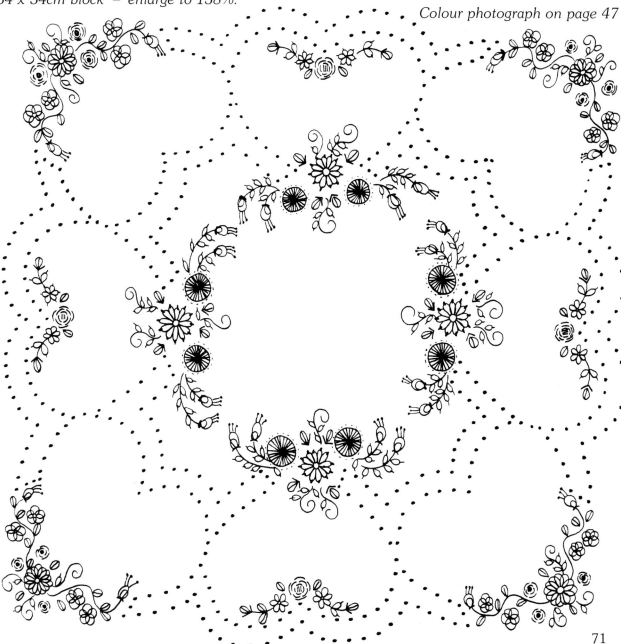

TULIP TIME

*Colour photograph
on page 47*

*To make the design on
this page fit a
34 x 34cm block
– enlarge to
143%.*

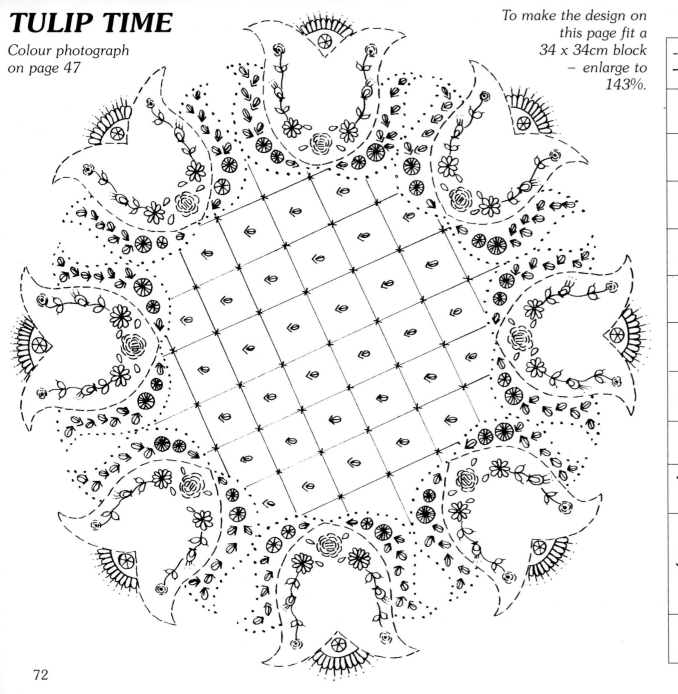

	COUCHING – cream with green cross
	OLD ENGLISH BUD – shades of pink and green
	BUTTONHOLE PINWHEEL FLOWER – bright pink/blue
	LAZY DAISY FLOWER – bright pink
	SWEET ROSE BUD – shades of pink
	LOOPED BUD – shades of bright pink/blue
	GRUB ROSE – shades of rose pink and bright pink
	LAZY DAISY FERN – green
	WHIPPED SPIDER'S WEB – blue/ bright pink
	TULIP OUTLINE – WHIPPED BACKSTITCH – alternating pink and blue
	CENTRE – WHIPPED SPIDER'S WEB – blue/bright pink Area around centre – FRENCH KNOTS – yellow and pink **PETALS** – LAZY DAISY with EXTENDED FRENCH KNOTS – yellow and pink
	COLONIAL KNOTS – cream

STITCH GLOSSARY

Stem Stitch
Running Stitch
Laced Running Stitch
Back Stitch
Whipped Backstitch
Basic Chain Stitch
Detached Chain (Lazy Daisy)
Double Lazy Daisy
Bullion – Lazy Daisy Combination
Whipped Chain Stitch
Buttonhole Stitch

Wheatear Stitch
Straight or Stab Stitch
Cast-on Buttonhole Stitch
Couching
Coral Stitch
Pekinese Stitch
Tufting
Fly Stitch
Romanian Stitch
Feather Stitch
Cretan Stitch

Woven Picot
Woven Spider's Web
Whipped Spider's Web
Raised Stem Stitch
French Knots
Extended French Knots
Colonial Knot
Bullion
Looped Bullion

=== A NOTE TO LEFT-HANDED EMBROIDERERS: ===

Look at the stitch in a mirror or make a photocopy of the stitch, hold the paper
up to the light on the reverse side and sketch your own left-handed stitch.

STEM STITCH

Work from the left to the right, keeping the thread to the left of the needle and making small, even stitches By repeating this stitch you can fill an area. When stem stitch is used to attach an appliqué design, it is often referred to as outline stitch.

RUNNING STITCH

Bring the thread through to the front on the line of your design. Pass the needle over and under the fabric. Make the top stitches of equal length and the under stitches equal but only half as long. It can be used as a single row or worked in rows to form a pattern.

LACED RUNNING STITCH

In a contrasting colour and using a blunt needle weave your thread from one side to the other. Do not pick up any fabric when weaving.

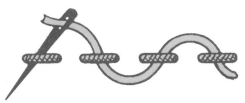

BACK STITCH

Bring your thread through to the front of your work on the line of your design. Take a small stitch backwards then bring your needle up a stitch's width in front of the first stitch. Now continue in this fashion going back to the previous stitch and coming up forward of the last stitch.

This stitch is used for fine lines and stems.

WHIPPED BACKSTITCH

Work from right to left. Use a blunt needle or the back of your needle and contrasting thread. Come up at the start of your design and whip your thread over and under each stitch. Take care not to pick up any fabric. Other stitches which can be whipped are chain stitch and stem stitch.

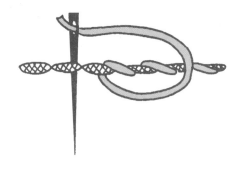

BASIC CHAIN STITCH

Bring the thread through the fabric. Hold the thread to the left making a loop shape. Reinsert the needle at the starting point, bring it out again a short distance away and take it over the loop of the thread. Pull through. Repeat the loop, inserting the needle exactly where the thread came out, inside the previous loop.

Chain stitch can be used as a filler if it is worked in continuous rows. Always work in the same direction, begining each new row at the same end.

DETACHED CHAIN (LAZY DAISY)

Work a single chain stitch and anchor it with a small straight stitch. Five small, detached chain stitches arranged like a flower make a daisy – hence the name.

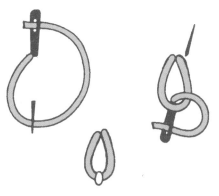

DOUBLE LAZY DAISY

This stitch can be worked in 2 colours – work the inner chain stitch first and the 2nd one around that. Uses: petals and leaves.

BULLION – LAZY DAISY COMBINATION

Bring the thread through to the top of your fabric and come up at the inner side of your design. Insert the needle as if you were going to make a single chain stitch. [Thread below your needle] Now instead of pulling the needle through, wrap the thread ¾ times around it's point . Support the wraps on the needle, and pull the needle through. Insert the needle at the tip of the bullion and push through to the back to anchor the stitch. Uses: petals and leaves.

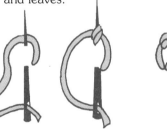

WHIPPED CHAIN STITCH

Make a foundation row of chain stitch. Using a contrasting thread, pass the thread over and under each link of the chain without penetrating the fabric.

BUTTONHOLE STITCH

Bring your thread to the top of the fabric on the outside edge of your design. Work from left to right or anti clockwise. Insert your needle on the inner edge and come out on the outer edge, making sure that the thread is held down under your needle. Pull the needle through and make the next stitch, spacing them evenly in a line or working in a circle.

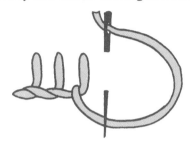

WHEATEAR STITCH

Another delightful foliage stitch. Make two straight stitches (a) and (b). Bring the thread through the fabric a small distance below these two stitches at (c) and pass the needle under the two stitches without entering the fabric. Close the chain at (c) and come out again at (d) to begin the "ear" of wheat.

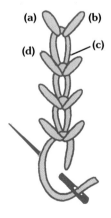

STRAIGHT OR STAB STITCH

Bring your thread to the right side of your fabric and work a stitch to where it is required.

These can be worked evenly, or unevenly to give a short and long effect. Do not make them too long or they tend to catch or get pulled.

CAST-ON BUTTONHOLE STITCH

With this stitch you cast-on as you do for knitting. Bring the thread up to the top of the fabric. Now prepare a backstitch but do not pull the needle through the fabric. Wrap the thread over your left index and thumb, twist it and cast it on to your needle. Do this as many times as required trying to keep an even tension. To avoid casting one stitch on top of the other tighten each stitch as you cast it on to the needle and then slide it down to the base. When you have cast on enough times, pull the needle through and anchor the stitch by inserting the needle into the fabric and through to the back. When making a looped cast-on buttonhole take a very small back stitch, and when anchoring the loop push the needle through to the back very close to where it originally emerged.

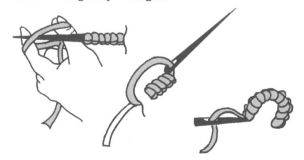

COUCHING

Lay one thread down along the line of the design. With a second thread [can be a contrast] catch this thread down making a little stitch through the fabric at equal intervals.

CORAL STITCH

Work from right to left. Bring the thread to the front of your fabric. Lay it along the line of your design. Take a stitch under the line and the thread and pull through to form a knot. The needle must pass over the lower thread in order to form the knot.

PEKINESE STITCH

This is another decorative weaving stitch. Make a foundation row of backstitch and then, working from the left, weave through the backstitches forming a braid like effect. You can use the same colour or a contrast thread.

TUFTING

This stitch is used to fill an area and resembles a carpet pile. The stitches should be worked as close together as possible. Start on the top side of your fabric and take a small stitch, leaving a loop of thread ±1cm long. To secure that loop, make a tiny backstitch at the base of your loop. Fill the entire area in this manner. When you cannot squeeze another stitch into the area go through to the back and end off. With a sharp pair of scissors cut the loops off creating a flat, even pile.

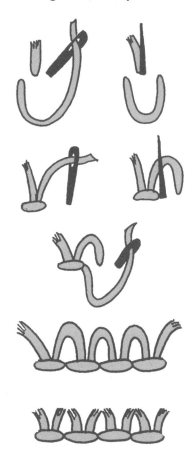

FLY STITCH

Bring the thread up at the top left point and hold the thread down – insert your needle to the right at the same level and take a diagonal stitch to the centre and downwards. Pull through. Make sure your thread is below the needle. To anchor, either make a small straight stitch or, for the extended fly stitch, make a *long* straight stitch. Work fly stitches in singles or vertically in a row, or in a circle to make flowers.

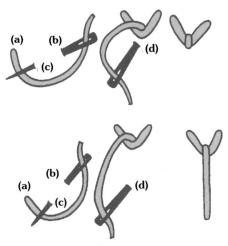

ROMANIAN STITCH

Bring your thread through at the top left of the shape. Carry your thread across and take a stitch on the right side of the shape keeping the thread below the needle. Come up in the centre, and anchor the bar. Now take a stitch to the left side. Work these 2 stitches until the shape is filled. Uses: mostly on leaves.

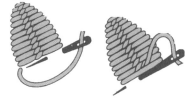

FEATHER STITCH

Bring thread up to the front of your fabric on the design line. Keeping the thread held down, insert your needle a little to the right on the same level. Take a diagonal stitch, coming out on the design line. Pull through. Now repeat this from the left side – always keeping the thread below the needle. Work these two stitches alternately. You may also work 2 stitches from the right and then 2 from the left to give a double feather stitch.

CRETAN STITCH

Bring thread through just off centre, taking a small stitch, needle pointing inwards and with thread under the needle point, as shown at (a). Take a stitch from the opposite side , thread under the needle as shown at (b). Continue in this way until the shape is filled.

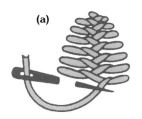 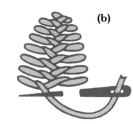

WOVEN PICOT

Make three spokes or stab stitches wider at one end and tapering at the tip. There must be an uneven number of stitches. With another thread, coming up at the tip of one of the outer stab stitches, weave back and forth, over and under the stab stitches.

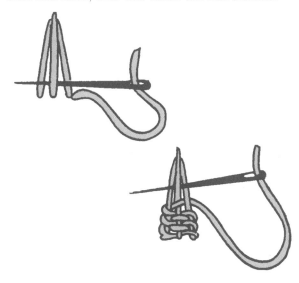

WOVEN SPIDER'S WEB

Make 5/7 spokes or stab stitches. [Must be an uneven number] Start by coming up in the centre, and then weave over and under your stab stitches around and around until the stab stitches or spokes are totally covered.

WHIPPED SPIDER'S WEB

In the circle make 8 even straight stitches radiating outwards. Now bring your thread up in the centre, in the V of 2 stitches. Working anti-clockwise go back over the spoke [straight stitch] to the right and under it and the next spoke to the left. Now pull your thread up tightly towards the centre. Repeat this, going around the centre until all your spokes are completely covered. You can make these webs multicoloured by starting with one colour and changing half way to another colour.

RAISED STEM STITCH

Make a ladder of stitches about a matchhead apart. Now working with a blunt needle or the back of your needle, taking care not to catch your fabric, start at one end of the ladder and work stem stitch from rung to rung as illustrated. Work row after row until the ladder is completely full. Always start at the same end of the ladder.

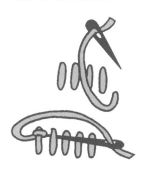 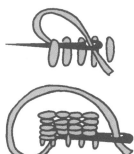

FRENCH KNOTS

Bring the needle through the fabric. Hold the thread taut with the left hand while wrapping the thread around the needle one or two times. Reinsert the needle close to where the thread emerged. French knots can be scattered like little seeds or used to fill an area. They are ideal for flower centres.

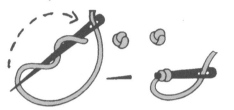

EXTENDED FRENCH KNOTS

Bring the needle through the fabric. Hold the thread taught and place the needle across the thread a small distance away from the exit point. Wrap the thread around the needle one or two times. Keeping the "stalk" taut, re-insert the needle at this point. The length of the stalk can vary.

BULLION

Bring the needle through to the top of your fabric and prepare a backstitch, the size of the bullion required but do not pull the needle through the fabric. The needle point should come out where the thread emerged from the bottom. Now twist the thread around the needle point as many times as required to equal the size of the backstitch. Support the coiled threads on the needle with two fingers and with your other hand pull the needle through. Now pull the knot back in the opposite direction. Pull the thread towards you to tighten it. It will now lie flat. Anchor your knot by making a stitch through to the back. Using a straw needle will help make even wraps.

COLONIAL KNOT

Pull the thread through the fabric. Place the needle under the thread, sliding the needle from left to right. (a) Wrap the thread over the top of the needle from right to left creating a figure eight. (b) Insert the needle into the fabric close to where it emerged; pull the working thread taut with your left hand so that a firm tight knot is formed. (c) Pull the needle to the wrong side of the fabric forming a colonial knot. Come up at the next dot (d).

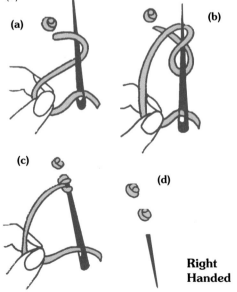

Right Handed

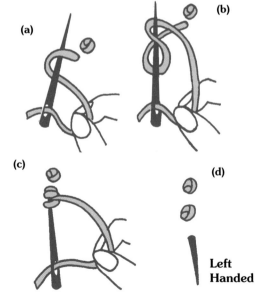

Left Handed

LOOPED BULLION:

When making your first stitch take up a minute amount of fabric. The bullion cannot lie flat as there is not enough fabric for it to do so, it thus makes a loop.